Steven McQuoid writes out of the con͏ͅ
needs a new generation of preachers'. ͏
potential to whet the spiritual appetite of such. A well-crafted manual
on preaching, it is surprisingly comprehensive for its size, and is marked
by practicality and realism. Both emerging and established preachers
cannot fail to profit from it.

Derek Prime
Author and former pastor of Charlotte Chapel, Edinburgh

Yet another book on preaching? Yes! For those who preach can never
receive enough instruction, stimulation and encouragement in their
work. And few things are more stimulating to preachers than listening
to or reading what a fellow-preacher has to say on this great subject.
Stephen McQuoid's readily digestible and stimulating new book will
help seasoned preachers (and enable them to give themselves a good
check-up). Beginners will benefit from the straightforward and sensible
counsel he gives. And some who never preach may be helped to pray
for and encourage those who do. So, I for one am grateful for the
labour of love this little manual represents and warmly welcome it.

Sinclair B. Ferguson
Associate Preacher, St Peter's Free Church, Dundee

This is a great little book for potential preachers, lay preachers, divinity
students and indeed experienced ministers of the Word. Stephen
McQuoid shares his own preaching experience to great effect as he
firmly roots the importance of preaching biblically and historically and
practically.

It is a book for preachers by a preacher. Young men studying for
the ministry would do very well to take note of what is written in the
book regarding the importance of knowing the biblical text. As they
also recognise tools of the trade and appreciate the value of putting
effort into the style and presentation of sermons, they will greatly
improve their preaching. In many ways, the book reminded me of a
shortened, updated version of *Lectures to my Students* by CH Spurgeon.

The need for good preachers today is a key sentiment that I heartily
endorse. It is not enough for the church to pray for more preachers –
we need more of the best! We need men with a real sense of calling,
with the appropriate gifts, and with a willingness to learn and develop

their trade. We need preachers who communicate to the highest standard – and this book will help.

Stephen McQuoid will succeed in making preachers think hard about the passion, preparation, style and development of their preaching gift. I trust it will be a blessing and a challenge to them – it certainly was for me.

Derek Lamont
Pastor, St Columba's Free Church of Scotland, Edinburgh

This is a primer on preaching. Naturally one cannot expect a relatively short book to comprehensively deal with all the issues. But as an introduction to the subject from an author who passionately believes in the value of preaching it is distilled common sense.

Its great strength is the emphasis placed on preaching accurately: relaying what is in the text and the passage rather than bending the text to suit the preacher's convenience – a cardinal sin unblushingly committed in many pulpits up and down the land! McQuoid gives an excellent summary on the all important subject of hermeneutics – how to understand and interpret Scripture in its original setting and then proceed on a fast track down two thousand years in order to apply the text or passage's abiding principles to contemporary times without perpetrating an exegetical injustice.

Dr Tony Sargent
Principal Emeritus, International Christian College, Glasgow

The Beginner's Guide to Expository Preaching

Stephen McQuoid

CHRISTIAN
FOCUS

Stephen McQuoid is the principal of Tilsley College, which is part of the ministry of Gospel Literature Outreach. He teaches theology and evangelism at the college and has a preaching ministry which takes him throughout Britain and abroad. Along with his wife Debbie, he is involved in a church planting work in Viewpark, Uddingston. Stephen is the author of *A New Kind of Living*, and *God's Family* and *Sharing the Good News in C21*.

© Copyright Stephen McQuoid 2002

ISBN 978-1-85792-769-6

Published in 2002
Reprinted 2014
by
Christian Focus Publications, Ltd.
Geanies House, Fearn, Tain,
Ross-shire, IV20 1TW, Great Britain.

www.christianfocus.com

Cover Design by Alister MacInnes

Printed and bound by CPI Group (UK) Ltd, Croydon, CR0 4YY

• Contents •

Preface and Acknowledgements   7

Part I : Preach the Word

1. The Biblical and Historical Basis of Preaching   9
2. Preaching Under Siege   17
3. In Defence of Preaching   27
4. Defining the Job   33

Part II: Ancient Text, Modern Setting

5. The Art of Reading the Bible   47
6. Language, History and Culture   55
7. Understanding Genre   67
8. Tools of the Trade   97

Part III: The House that Exposition Built

9. Putting it All Together   109
10. Introduction and Conclusion   119
11. Opening Windows   133
12. The Presentation   143
13. Preach the Word   153

Appendix 1: Practising your Introduction   157
Appendix 2 : Practising your Illustrations   158
Appendix 3: Preaching Assessment Sheet   159
Endnotes   161
Bibliography   168

• Preface •

There is an old adage that says, 'Those who can, do, and those who can't, teach'. I think this could be rephrased so that it states, 'Those who can, do, those who can't, write books about it'. My reason for writing a book on preaching was not because I think of myself as a brilliant preacher. Indeed, though I preach regularly, I am constantly reminded of my limited gift. I am just one of the many 'ministers of the word' who work hard so as to communicate something of God's truth to those who listen.

So why write about preaching? Actually I have three reasons. Firstly, I love teaching or training others so that they can serve God more effectively. That is why I have spent the past twelve years of my life lecturing at Tilsley College. This book was designed as a practical introduction to the art of preaching. Secondly, I believe there is a huge need today for passionate, biblical preaching. This book came out of a deep desire to encourage others to give themselves to this great work. Thirdly, I have had the privilege of hearing many great preachers and have consciously tried to note what makes them so good (other than the fact that they are anointed by God). In this book I have attempted to summarise some of those key things so that others may benefit as I have.

There are a number of people I would like to thank as they have directly or indirectly contributed to this book. First and foremost I must thank my wife, Debbie, who puts up with the long hours that I work and is the most honest critic of my preaching, as well as my greatest supporter. I would also pay tribute to friends who have inspired me with their love of Scripture, not least my father who helped me construct my very first sermon. A special thanks to Jim Brown for proofreading the manuscript. I must also thank the staff at Tilsley College for their fellowship and the many stimulating conversations we have together. In particular I would single out my friend and colleague Allison Hill who makes my job so much easier by doing hers so very well.

I must also thank two groups of people. Firstly, the students at Tilsley College who sat through my lectures on preaching. It was in these classes that the material for this book came together and the feedback from those students has been of great value. Secondly, the members of the preaching group in my own church, Viewpark Christian Fellowship. It was in this group that the material for this book was refined and put into an accessible format. Thank you all.

It is my prayer that this book will enable its readers to preach a little better and in doing so contribute to the health of the church.

The Biblical and Historical Basis of Preaching

I can remember as a boy being taken along to church. The songs were alright, the people friendly and the atmosphere generally warm. As for the sermons, I confess I could not see the point. Was it because I was so young? Perhaps it was because the preachers sometimes went over their time? Or maybe it was a combination of both. Whatever the reasons, my attitude was excusable on account of my tender years and lack of spiritual insight. What is less excusable, however, is the negative press that sermons get in the life of some contemporary churches.

Not all Christians today are enthralled with the idea of the 'Sunday Sermon'. For reasons that will be investigated later, some Christians feel that preaching has had its day and should now gracefully lie down and die in order to make way for other more interesting items in the church programme. I must state emphatically that this view flies in the face of both Scripture and church history.

Preaching in the Old Testament

Preaching, which is the job of declaring the Word of God, can be found as far back as Old Testament times. Some of the early leaders of the Old Testament believing community were preachers and they unashamedly declared God's Word to the people (Deut.32 ; Josh.23-

24). Even Moses, who felt utterly unable to speak, became a preacher (Ex.4:10-16). His protests on the issue were met with the reply that God would enable him to speak and teach him what to say. Despite his unwillingness, Moses became God's mouthpiece to the people.[1]

The Old Testament prophets carried on this mantle (Jer.11:6 ; Amos 7:14,15). Their sermons are different from today's in the sense that God was speaking through them in a particular way, inspiring them so that their words became Scripture. But there are also similarities between them and modern preachers. Firstly, they considered their job to be that of declaring God's Word, and all true preachers today do the same. As they spoke they conveyed what God was saying to his people, and that is the essence of the job of preaching, whether it was done in 2,000 BC or being done in 2,000 AD. Secondly, they challenged their audience to respond to God's Word, and encouraged them into a life of obedience. All true preaching makes this same appeal.

Though the words of the prophets became part of the canon of Scripture, and though the canon of Scripture is now closed, preaching today is based on Scripture. The Bible is our source of truth and is authoritative for all matters of faith and practice, the material from which contemporary preachers must draw their sermon content. In this sense, despite the unique role of the preachers of the Old Testament, we can join with them as in our own generation, we declare God's Word to modern day audiences.

Preaching in the New Testament
The New Testament is also full of preaching. Without

question the greatest preacher in the New Testament was Jesus himself. It is equally beyond doubt that preaching formed a crucial part of the ministry of Christ. Jesus seems to have begun his ministry by preaching in the open air (Mark 1:14) while in Galilee.[2] He then called his Disciples, began his ministry of healing, and again Mark comments that Jesus continued in the ministry of preaching (Mark 1:39). Luke tells us that Jesus saw preaching as his mission in life (Luke 4:43). It was for this reason that he was sent. We also read that he frequented synagogues (Matt. 9:35) again with the express purpose of preaching. It has been pointed out that synagogue addresses encouraged debate and even heated discussion and were therefore different in their presentation from much of contemporary preaching.[3] Nevertheless this was preaching in the true sense of the word.

Jesus did not see preaching as his work alone. He also wanted his followers to begin declaring the Word of God. In Mark 3:14 he appointed the Twelve so that he could send them out to preach. Later on we read that they then went out and preached everywhere (Mark 16:20). His burden and vision to convey God's Word to the world was being passed on to them.

It was clear from the very outset of the Christian church that preaching was seen as a crucial aspect of Christian discipleship. In Acts 6:2-4 the Apostles recognised that they were becoming so involved in practical caring for the church that the preaching of the Word was being neglected. They took action to ensure that this would not happen. It was not that they considered the work of caring for widows to be unimportant, quite the reverse, but they had such a high view of preaching that they considered it to be essential in the life of the church.

Paul was also a great champion of preaching. His ministry was full of it (Acts 15:35 ; 28:31). Like Jesus before him, Paul encouraged others to take up the responsibility of declaring God's Word. He told Timothy to find faithful men and train them up so they in turn would pass on God's message to others. He also left Timothy with the awesome responsibility to, *'preach the word ... in season and out of season'* (2 Tim. 4:1,2). Timothy was to commit himself to this ministry under all circumstances, whether it was convenient to do so or not.[4] Once again the priority of preaching was underlined.

The Church Fathers

Once we go beyond the end of the canon of Scripture we note that preaching continued to be an essential component of church life. In the second century Justin Martyr wrote his *First Apology* in defence of Christianity, addressing it to the emperor. He described a typical Sunday service and made the point that preaching was an essential part of this Christian gathering. He states that during a service, *'the memoirs of the apostles or writings of the prophets are read, as long as time permits; then, when the reader has ceased, the president verbally instructs, and exhorts to the imitation of these good things.'*[5]

Two centuries later Eusebius, Bishop of Caesarea, described the activities of the church from its inception. He mentioned the centrality of preaching in the life and experience of the church, describing the early Christians as people whose hearts were, *'smitten by the word of God'* and who were, *'ambitious to preach to those who had never yet heard the message*.[6] Towards the end of the fourth century, a giant of a preacher called John Chrysostom (lit. golden-mouth) emerged. John Stott notes that Chrysostom's preaching was characterised by its biblical content, its straightforward interpretation, its practical application and its fearlessness.[7] Chrysostom, who was the Bishop of Constantinople, said that preaching was the only thing that would cure diseases in the body of Christ. Clearly the ministry of Christ was still being imitated and the faithful preaching of the word of God was a key feature of Christian ministry.

The Reformation

When we come to the Reformation once again preaching features greatly. Luther, the great German reformer, became convinced not only of the primacy of Scripture, but of the need for it to be preached. In his church in Wittenberg, there were three services every Sunday and several during the week. Each of these included preaching within the programme. Luther himself had a heavy preaching ministry. His biographer, Roland Bainton, notes that, *'He (Luther) spoke often four times on Sundays and quarterly undertook a two week series four days a week on the catechism. The sum of his extant sermons is 2,300. The highest count is for the year 1528, for which there are 195 sermons distributed over 145 days'*.[8] Luther also gave advice on preaching which included the need to be willing to preach even in the face of great opposition and ridicule. There can be no doubt that Luther's preaching as well as his writings brought about the German Reformation.

Calvin demonstrated an equal commitment to preaching. In his *Institutes of Christian Religion* he endeavoured to sum up what it was that constituted a true church. His conclusion was that '*Wherever we see the Word of God purely preached...it is not to be doubted, a church of God exists*'. He repeated this assertion again stating that wherever a Christian gathering '*has the ministry of the Word and honours it...it deserves without doubt to be held and considered a church*'.[10]

The emphasis that the Reformers had on preaching has prompted many to comment that the pulpit was higher than the altar.[11] Preaching was without doubt a central pillar of the Reformation.

The Puritans and Beyond

The Puritans too were people who believed in preaching. Indeed they considered the sermon to be the climax of a worship service, something that was deeply honouring to God. For them a sermon was not something to be rushed, so brevity was not a feature for which they were noted. They were methodical in their preaching, working hard at sermon preparation, often writing out the whole sermon word for word. Their sermons were expository in nature, full of doctrine and very orderly. This did not mean, however, that Puritan preaching was dull and stodgy. Far from it! Their preaching was passionate, full of illustrations and they constantly applied the message to the lives of their hearers.[12]

One leading Puritan, Richard Baxter, wrote a book entitled 'The Reformed Pastor'. In it he encouraged his fellow ministers to preach faithfully. He lamented the fact that, '*few ministers do preach with all their might*' and urged his readers to, '*awaken your own hearts, before you go to the pulpit, that you may be fit to awaken the hearts of sinners*'.[13]

Following on from the Puritans came two men whose names are readily associated with preaching, John Wesley and George Whitefield. They were used powerfully to reach many for Christ and to build up the church. Both were passionate preachers and both saw preaching as fundamental to the work of God.

Whitefield, with his legendary energy managed to preach twenty sermons per week in a ministry that lasted more than thirty years. John Pollock recounts an amusing occasion when an old man fell asleep while Whitefield was preaching in a New Jersey meeting-house. Incensed Whitefield clapped his hands loudly and stamped his foot to wake the man up and declared, '*I have come to you in the name of the Lord God of Hosts and I must and I will be heard*'.[14] Such stories demonstrate the seriousness with which men like Whitefield took the ministry of preaching. A ministry so powerful that people were literally felled under its influence as the Holy Spirit used the spoken word.[15]

The Modern Era

Our modern era has also witnessed great preaching. Dr Martin Lloyd Jones, an assistant to Lord Thomas Horder, left his Harley Street practice to take up a pastorate at a small church in his native South Wales. Preaching was the great emphasis of his ministry and through preaching he saw the congregation grow from eighty worshippers to over five hundred.[16] From there he went to Westminister Chapel, London, where his preaching influenced literally thousands of people.

Billy Graham has also been used uniquely, particularly as an evangelistic preacher. Huge numbers of people have been drawn into a living relationship with

Jesus Christ through his ministry. Many Christian leaders today point to the great influence that Billy Graham's preaching ministry has had, not only on their own lives, but on the spiritual tone of whole nations.

All this must convey a powerful lesson to churches today. Preaching is biblical, and it is a means by which God has spoken since Old Testament times. God has used preaching to win countless millions of souls for Christ. God has also used preaching to encourage, correct and stimulate his church over the ages, so that Christians from all cultures and walks of life are spiritually enriched and activated for service. That being the case, preaching must be seen as a precious gem that should be treasured and used for the glory of God.

Summary:
- In the Old Testament, men of God like Moses and Amos preached the word and impacted the nation.
- Jesus preached and chose 'the twelve' so that they would be preachers also.
- The Church Fathers continued the ministry of preaching.
- Preaching was at the heart of the Reformation and the Puritan era.
- God still uses preaching today to touch the lives of millions.

Pause for Thought:
Spend time reading a biography of one of history's great preachers and ask yourself the question, what motivated this person to be a preacher?

2

Preaching Under Siege

Despite the biblical injunction to 'preach the word', and the fact that preaching has been used of God throughout the ages to challenge and encourage the church; despite the fact that millions have been brought into a closer walk with God as a result of the faithful proclamation of his Word, preaching is nevertheless an aspect of church life that is under siege.

The challenges to good preaching in today's church come from many different directions, both inside and outside the Christian community. Whenever an important aspect of church life is challenged, we need to acknowledge the challenge and confront it head on. So what are the challenges to good preaching? What obstacles will today's preacher face as he endeavours to declare God's Word to his contemporaries?

The TV Generation
Probably the most obvious challenge that confronts the modern preacher is that of the TV generation. Very rarely can we look back in church history and say that those who have gone before have not experienced what we are now experiencing. When it comes to the issue of the media, however, we can make this assertion with confidence. Never before have preachers had to face such a media saturated society. There has never been a time like the present, when the preacher has had to deal with

an audience that has been fed on a diet of soundbites and instant images.

In 1956 there were 15.6 million homes in Britain, but only 5.7 million of them had televisions. By 1998 the number of homes had increased to 24.3 million, and at the same time the number of homes with televisions increased to 23.6 million.[1] Today it is not hard to find a household with at least two TV's, a video, a sophisticated stereo system, a range of computer games and a link with the Internet. A MORI poll conducted in June 1996 revealed that eight out of ten teenagers (aged between 15 and 19 years) had a television in their bedroom.[2] Not only has television become a universal medium for receiving information, the use of video has also increased over the past few years. Though the percentage of homes with a video varies depending on socio-economic grouping, statistics reveal that 91per cent of 'professional' households possess a video, while 66 per cent of 'economically inactive' have one.[3]

Television viewing has become the nation's most popular pasttime. Statistics released in August 1999 reveal that the average television viewing time per person in Britain was a massive 23 hours and 15 minutes per week.[4] That works out at over three hours per day. The age bracket most likely to watch a lot of television are those who have retired. Of the 65 and over age group the average viewing per person is 35 hours per week for men and 37 hours per week for women.[5] People who are working and have family responsibilities are still liable to spend significant amounts of time in front of the television. Those aged between 25 and 44 watch over 20 hours of television per week.[6]

Gone are the days when young people spent the bulk of their recreational time playing football, chatting together or participating in some kind of group activity. Though much of this still exists, an increasing amount of time is being spent watching television and videos, playing on a games console, or surfing the net. What kind of people will this intimacy with the small screen produce?

Firstly, it produces people with a short attention span. Most television commercials last only a few seconds, yet they communicate sufficiently to sell their products. Any documentary, film or even news bulletin will change camera angle and move swiftly from one item to the next to keep the viewers' attention. People are accustomed to concentrating on something for just a few minutes at the most. This makes the job of the preacher harder as he essentially stands and talks for a protracted period of time. This is probably the only time in the week that many of the members of his congregation will just sit and listen, concentrating on only one thing for more than twenty minutes.

Secondly, it produces people who are uncritical of what they take in. Television has an educational value, but it is mostly used for entertainment. The purpose of most television programmes is not to stimulate the mind into reasoning through some pertinent issue, but to enable the viewer to relax and enjoy. This in itself is not wrong, but it does mean that viewers get into the habit of just absorbing information without dialogue, response or critical evaluation. What is more, this can potentially produce a world in which morally questionable things are accepted as the norm.

Many soap operas, films and dramas portray a world in which sex before marriage is uncomplicated and morally neutral, a world which does not distinguish between heterosexual and homosexual relationships. Many infer that violence is appropriate and even fun and that rebellion and law- breaking is heroic. Some even encourage the viewer to take a voyeuristic pleasure in the misery and heartache of the hapless and the vulnerable. A constant diet of this material desensitises the conscience and breeds an attitude of uncritical acceptance.

I am not for a moment condemning the watching of television. I watch TV and enjoy it. I am well aware of the benefits that television has brought to the lives of many. Nevertheless, with the lack of censorship which pervades the media, and with people watching so much of it, we are being unrealistic if we assume that it will have no effect on the minds, attitudes and emotional wellbeing of the people in our congregation. More and more people have their personal morality shaped by Oprah Winfrey, Rikki Lake and Jerry Springer. Increasing people accept that what they see on the small screen is not only the norm, but acceptable. Many Christians will spend twice as much time watching television as they do studying the Bible, or listening to it being taught and discussed. This will clearly influence them and impinge on their judgment.

This challenge needs to be faced up to. Today's preacher needs to hold the concentration of his audience. This may involve using a variety of styles in his preaching, the use of good illustrations and visual aids, and being creative in his presentation. He also needs to preach in such a way as to make his audience think about the message and evaluate it. There is no point in preaching if it goes in one ear of his listeners and then immediately out the other. His preaching must provoke thought and a response. He must also preach such spiritually enriching sermons that they actively combat the permissive attitudes which his listeners have imbibed in this television centred culture.

Individualism

Another significant barrier that challenges the modern preacher is that of individualism. We live in a society where people are used to doing what they want, where autonomy is seen as a virtue and conformism is sneered at. People do not as a whole enjoy rules, whether it is keeping to the speed limits on our roads or simply waiting our turn in a queue. Something within all of us wants to be in charge so that we can make our own decisions about life.

The job of the preacher is to declare 'thus saith the Lord'. What we preach is not a matter of opinion, neither is it something that can be negotiated. The Word of God is to be obeyed. In that sense the preacher is telling his audience how they must behave and what they must do, and he does so with an authority that is invested in his ministry by Almighty God. He is expecting that his audience will follow God's will and not their own. This will of course mean that the preaching of the Word of God will come up against the individual's desire for self-determination. Such a clash can provoke a response and make preaching unpopular.

Today's preacher must face up to the individualism of our culture and challenge it, despite the unpopularity of such an approach. He is not in a popularity contest or running around kissing babies like a politician desperate for votes. He is an emissary from God delivering a message which all must obey, however independent they may wish to be. His job is not to pander to individual egos, but to challenge all to obey.

Concept of Truth

A third barrier that the preacher faces is the erosion of the concept of truth in contemporary society. One of the most dramatic results of post-modernity is it's questioning of truth as an absolute. In previous generations people accepted that there were absolutes, that truth could be objective and culture transcending. Today the talk is of 'your truth' and 'my truth'. If we say to someone that we are sharing something that is true they might reply by saying 'it may be true for you but it is not true for me'.

For Christians the truth of the Word of God is absolute and irrevocable. It is not something that can be compromised, neither is it just true for some people. Rather it is true for all people in every culture. Preaching is the declaration of this truth to all who listen. But in preaching in this way we come into conflict with a world view that says that truth is personal, subjective and certainly not universal.

That does not mean that our preaching should stop or be modified to fit in with the fallen-ness of popular culture. Far from it, the Word of God must be declared. At the same time, this errant concept of truth does provide a significant challenge to the declaration of God's truth. This challenge must be met with a declaration of God's Word in which the preacher explicitly states that

Scripture is truth in an absolute sense and that it cannot be relativised.

The Instant Word

Yet another challenge facing the preacher is that of the 'instant word'. With the resurgence of the use of spiritual gifts in the life of the church over the past few decades, the potential for imbalance and extremes has arisen. We should be thankful to God for the renewed vigour with which many Christians and churches are exercising their spiritual gifts. At the same time some churches have been guilty of over emphasising some gifts at the expense of others. One of the most neglected gifts, in my judgment, is that of preaching.

In particular it has been a feature of some churches to show a preference for the instant Word from God rather than the exposition of Scripture, to prefer prophecy to preaching. I am not in any way invalidating the gift of prophecy, or indeed any other spiritual gift, neither am I disassociating it from preaching. I am not questioning the value of prophecy either. But I have known of churches that have become so absorbed with the 'instant word' that they have completely shelved their preaching programme. This is clearly dangerous! Preaching may involve hard work and discipline, but it must be the staple diet of a local church.

As we use the spiritual gifts that God has given us, we must have a balanced approach, unlike the Corinthians who were told by Paul to grow up (1Corinthians 14:20). If this balance is to be maintained, preaching must be at the very centre of all that we do, the linchpin of the church programme. Without it our church life will rapidly become unhinged.

Marginalization of the Sermon in Church Life

A further obstacle which the modern preacher faces is the marginalization of the sermon in the life of the church. In reality few churches want to get rid of preaching altogether lest they be accused of throwing the baby out with the bath water. Many churches, however, are squeezing the sermon into an increasingly limited time slot so that it becomes an appendix to the church service rather than a focal point. On one recent occasion I was invited by a church to preach at their main Sunday service. The service itself lasted for an hour, but the time which was allocated to me for the sermon was twelve minutes. This I found alarming.

Church services are often busy events. Worship has become an increasingly important feature and this is evidenced by the huge number of praise songs which are being penned by contemporary songwriters. Drama and children's items are also very common. All these innovations are both good and helpful and have their place, but not at the expense of preaching. In reality, however, the sermon is often a lower priority than almost anything else.

The temptation to banish the sermon to the sidelines of church life in favour of more interesting items must be resisted strongly. The fact is that even if the members of a congregation do not recognise that they need to hear the Word of God expounded, they do! Without preaching they will suffer from spiritual malnutrition. They will then be susceptible to a whole range of spiritual diseases which might even cause complete spiritual paralysis and blindness.

The Monster of Laziness

One final obstacle which all preachers need to do battle with is the monster of laziness. Good preaching is the result of very hard work. It is 5 percent inspiration and 95 percent perspiration. We are all tempted to take shortcuts and church life can be very pressurised. Those preachers who also hold down secular jobs find the burden of preaching particularly heavy to bear. On top of a career which relentlessly demands more and more of their time and energy, they must summon the strength to prepare for the fast approaching Sunday service.

Preparing little and preaching light has often been considered an option, but it must not be. Such is the importance of good preaching that every effort must be made to ensure its quality. The preacher must put in the hours, make the effort, and like the apostles, prioritise, so that the declaration of the Word of God is not devoured by anything, not even the ferocious monster of laziness.

Summary:

*   The impact of TV has made the preacher's job much more difficult. He has to work hard to keep his audience's attention.
*   The individualism of our society makes it difficult for preaching to illicit obedience.
*   The changing concept of truth means that people will question the authority of Scripture.
*   Preachers will be tempted to take the easy option of the 'instant word' rather than the hard graft of study.
*   The sermon is increasingly marginalized in the life of many church services.

- Laziness leads to little preparation for sermons, which leads to a poor spiritual diet.

Pause for Thought:

Which of the dangers mentioned in this chapter is the biggest threat in the life of your church? What practical things can you do to counteract the danger?

3

In Defence of Preaching

In the previous chapter I pointed out some of the obstacles that the contemporary preacher has to face. These are considerable and need to be reckoned with. All the objections raised conspire to make preaching a less than popular notion.

But there is another threat which the preacher faces and this one comes from within the ranks of the Christian community. Some would argue that although the Word of God does need to be declared, there are more efficient ways of doing it than by preaching. They suggest that a monologue approach, which is typical in preaching, is rather outdated. That preaching is simply not a relevant form of communication in today's world. For many, conversational bible studies and group discussions are a much better way of communicating divine truth. Preaching, they will say, has had its day and should go gracefully into retirement.

To a degree I have a certain sympathy with this argument and recognise that it does arise as a result of listening to preaching at its worst. Frankly there have been times when I have been bored having to listen to long, dry sermons. There have also been occasions when I have left a church service feeling that I really did not learn very much. I am also committed to small bible study groups and in my own church, house groups play a crucial role in our teaching programme. But before we become too dismissive about preaching, I would like to point out the great benefits that preaching offers to the church and its timeless significance.

In saying this I am not advocating a stodgy diet of forty-five minute monologues devoid of character and interest. I don't enjoy bad preaching any more than anyone else. We do need to remember the short attention span which our audience will have. I am also in favour of creativity in the pulpit, using different styles and at times even an interactive approach which encourages a measure of audience participation. It is important to study and use good communication techniques in our preaching.

The point I must stress, however, is that preaching is a form of communication which is as invaluable now as it has been in the life of the church over the past two millennia. There are a number of reasons why I make this statement.

No better way of communicating to the whole church

Firstly, I believe that there is no better way of communicating to the whole church than by preaching. The beauty of a sermon is that it can be delivered to a large audience and this ensures that the whole church can learn at the same time. While home groups and study groups have their place, they are by their very nature, exclusive to the membership of the small group that meets.

Not so with preaching! Every one can be included and the church as a whole can experience and hear the voice of God. In this way church members can learn together and grow together as a whole body. Preaching therefore has a unifying effect as the whole church is brought under the sound of God's Word.

No better way of communicating the depths of Scripture to the church

A second benefit that preaching offers is that it can make available to the church some of the deep truths of Scripture. The Bible is a sizable book with many themes, literary genre and historical contexts. Reading is beneficial, but detailed study will bear even more fruit. While it is true that a child can understand much of Scripture and that the Holy Spirit ministers in the lives of Christians so that they can understand what they read, yet there will always be more to discover.

Any preacher worth his salt will be someone who studies the Bible in depth and communicates that depth to his audience. His audience will therefore benefit from the hours he has spent in the study, praying and in preparation. Invigorating discussions in small bible study groups are of great benefit, but they should not be at the expense of listening to a gifted preacher who has studied the passage in depth and thought about it at length. Preaching is not just sharing an opinion, however biblically based it might be. It is declaring what God has said so that the audience can understand its rich implications. Good preaching will deliver an insight into the Scriptures which will otherwise be inaccessible to most of our church members.

No better way of communicating the spirit of a text

A third benefit of preaching is that it can communicate not only the meaning of a text, but the spirit of a text as well. The Bible is a very dramatic book full of strongly expressed emotions. Imagine the tension which must have existed between Amos and Amaziah as they stood together in Bethel deliberating over Amos' pronouncements of judgment (Amos 7:10-17). Picture the faces of the crowd who looked with amazement as Jesus delivered the radical Sermon on the Mount. Try and capture how Paul felt as he penned the moving words of the letter to the Philippians from his prison cell. This is high drama indeed!

There is a very real sense in which preaching is a performance. Not that the preacher is looking for adulation or an Oscar, but it is a performance in the sense that the preacher needs to create an atmosphere in which the audience can understand not only what the biblical writers wrote, but why they wrote, and the emotions they felt at the time. There is no better way of recreating the drama and thrust of a biblical passage than to preach it with passion.

No better way of motivating a church into action

A fourth benefit of preaching is its motivational quality. There are few things in the Christian life more stirring than an impassioned sermon. My own experience and that of many people has been that at key moments in my own Christian development, God has used preaching to invigorate my faith and stimulate me into action.

A sermon is a rallying cry motivating the church to obey and serve God. It appeals for action and a changed life. It always anticipates that the hearer will respond and it points in the direction that the hearer should go. Every good sermon will give God's comment on any given situation and demonstrate God's answer. Good preaching will therefore keep a church on its toes and prevent spiritual complacency from sneaking in.

Summary:

- There is no better way of communicating to the whole church than by preaching.
- There is no better way of communicating the depths of Scripture to the whole church than by preaching.
- There is no better way of communicating the spirit of the text than by preaching.
- There is no better way of motivating the church into action than by preaching.

Pause for Thought:

Given the enormous benefits of preaching, what practical steps can you take to ensure that preaching in not only at the centre of the life of your church, but also valued by the congregation?

4

Defining the Job

Having defended preaching, it is now important to define what the role of a preacher is. Definition always gives focus and without it we will never be able to do justice to the job. Many preachers are less effective than they should be simply because they have not thought carefully about what their job entails. Given the importance of the job of preaching, this is a tragedy.

Perhaps the best way of defining the job of a preacher is to begin by stating what a preacher's job is not. This will make us aware of the pitfalls which we need to avoid and provide a framework into which we can place a definition.

Not an Entertainer

Firstly, it must be stressed that a preacher is not an entertainer. Perhaps this point does not need to be made, but timely reminders of possible errors are never out of place.

I enjoy humour and even enjoy humour in the pulpit. A witty comment can often make a powerful point. It can also make a preacher increasingly easy to listen to which is no bad thing. That being said, however, the primary role of a preacher is not to be funny. It is not even to be interesting! Hopefully most preachers are interesting and are able to use humour appropriately. But that is not their job! Preachers are not primarily in the business of providing entertainment or amusing their congregation with a good day out each Sunday.

Some years ago I worked with one preacher who was extremely funny and a great communicator. I enjoyed his humour and loved hearing him preach because his presentation was so alive and absorbing. As time went on, however, it became obvious to me that the audience response to his humour was so positive that he fell into the trap of increasing the humour in his sermons, but decreasing the real biblical content. It was only a matter of time before his preaching had become a series of jokes with an occasional verse thrown in. His audiences got used to this diet, which was of little benefit to their spiritual development.

One day, he ended up preaching on a passage of Scripture that had a very serious message, and to his credit decided not to use any humour as it would have been inappropriate. His sermon was powerful, sobering and deeply challenging. The problem was that people simply weren't listening because it was devoid of the entertainment value which they were used to. Such are the pitfalls of preachers who try first and foremost to entertain.

Not a Scratcher

Secondly, a preacher is not there to scratch people's backs (or ears) simply telling them what they want to hear. This was the error that Paul warned Timothy against (2 Tim.4:3). It may well be that when we preach we often say things that are encouraging and make our audience feel good. Nothing is worse than a preacher who is always negative. But sermons are not primarily about the 'feel good' factor. That should only be the outcome if the passage being preached is meant to have that effect. But making people feel good about themselves is not the main function of preaching.

Not a Storyteller

Thirdly, preaching is not just about telling stories. The Bible of course is full of stories and they are great to listen to. Some are intriguing, some funny, some profoundly moving and some are even terrifying. Sometimes when illustrating a point you will also have to tell stories of your own. This is simply good communication. But if the stories, especially your own ones, take over, then the content of your sermon can be drowned in the flood of analogy. This is not what preaching is about. Preaching involves stories, but it is not just about storytelling.

If these words of caution provide a framework within which we can place a definition of preaching, then what should that definition be? The simplest, and one of the best definitions, states that preaching is **DECLARING THE WORD OF GOD TO MEN**. This definition does not sound very grand, but in a nutshell it encapsulates the essence of what preaching is all about. There are three points to note in this definition. Firstly, preaching involves the Word of God. Without the Bible there would be no preaching, for we would have no message to preach. Preaching therefore must be based on Scripture. To leave the Bible out is to make the sermon null and void, a mere reciting of powerless words.

Secondly, the definition involves declaration. We do not apologise for what the Bible says. Neither do we attempt to negotiate with it in order to get a better deal. What God says is what we declare. It is absolute truth, it is a message from God. The job of the preacher is to declare it and to do so in a way that demands a response. If those we are preaching to refuse to obey, that is between them and God. Our job as preachers is to declare what God is saying through his Word and urge a response of obedience.

Thirdly, preaching is aimed at people. Some of our preaching may be evangelistic and aimed at those who have not made any commitment to the person of Jesus Christ. Much of our preaching will be aimed at Christians. But all preaching is aimed at people, and is intended to be a communication from God to them, eliciting a response.

Expository Preaching

Having provided a basic definition of preaching, we now need to think a little more closely about what is actually involved in declaring God's Word to men. This leads us to an important word, the word 'expository'. Some would argue that the only kind of preaching is expository preaching. Certainly preaching in its purest and best form is expository. The best definition I have come across for expository preaching comes from Haddon Robinson.

> Expository preaching is the communication of a biblical concept, derived from and transmitted through a historical, grammatical, and literary study of a passage in its context, which the Holy Spirit first applies to the personality and experience of the preacher, then through him to his hearers.[1]

This definition gives us more to chew on. It also demonstrates why expository preaching is the best way of communicating what God is saying through his Word.

The expository method ensures that the passage of Scripture itself determines the content of the sermon. I have heard preachers who have read a Bible passage and then preached a sermon that only superficially touches on what the passage says. Clearly they had something that they wanted to say and then looked for a passage to justify their ideas or give them credibility. The content of their sermons were controlled, not by what the Bible says, but by what they wanted their audiences to hear. I have also heard preachers who randomly take verses out of their context for much the same reason. With this methodology Bible verses can easily be taken out of context and used to prove anything.

Expository preaching does not function like that. An expository sermon will investigate a biblical passage and express what the Bible actually says. The passage will therefore determine what is preached and the preacher will have no freedom to incorporate anything that is not clearly stated in the passage. Exposition also requires the preacher to interpret the passage, properly taking into consideration the literary and historical background and the specifics of the grammar. In this way the accurate meaning of the passage is discovered through diligent study.

This obviously involves a great deal of work. It is much easier just to read the occasional verse and interlace it with all kinds of stories and illustrations to keep the audience's attention. But if the Bible really is the Word of God, and if every word is inspired and there for a purpose, it must be taken seriously. As preachers we have a responsibility to God to accurately communicate what he is saying to mankind, and a responsibility to men to tell them what God has already said to them. Expository preaching is therefore the best kind of preaching, as it fulfils these obligations.

Preaching through Bible Books

The most obvious way of preaching a series of expository sermons is to take a Bible book and work systematically through it covering every verse. This has many advantages. To begin with, the individual books of the Bible came as a whole. Paul did not write a few isolated verses to the churches in Rome or Corinth. He wrote whole books. What is more, there is a logical progression of thought through each book and the thought flow is intrinsic to the meaning of the book. When the historical books of the Old Testament were penned they were not presented as a collection of short stories, but rather an historical account of God's consistent involvement in the lives of his people. Peaching through a book, therefore, will capture this continuity and greatly aid our understanding.

Preaching through a book will also enable us to cover some difficult subjects in a natural way. If I were to launch into a sermon on gossiping next Sunday, most of the people in my church would assume that there was some huge problem that I was trying urgently to address. Indeed, my sermon would cause a great deal of gossip in the church as everyone would openly speculate as to who was guilty of gossiping. If, on the other hand, I was preaching through the book of James, the issue of gossiping would emerge very naturally as part of the series and would not cause such a problem.

Preaching about Bible Characters

Clearly, preaching through a bible book is extremely beneficial and should be the norm for a church teaching programme. But there are other useful expository subjects. Preaching on the life of a bible character for instance. Biblical characters provide us with examples of how God deals with individuals. People find bible characters easy to identify with and when preaching about the life of a biblical character we can point out not only their successes, but their failures also.

Biblical characters are vivid and the Bible makes no attempt to gloss over their faults and shortcomings. Solomon is pictured as a wise fool, and David, the man after God's own heart, as someone who could fall into the sin of adultery. Abraham, the friend of God, also knew doubt while Peter was in the habit of saying the wrong thing at the wrong time. These were all real people who endeavoured to serve God despite their limitations and sinfulness. Their lives provide us with inspiration and lessons for living.

Preaching a Theme

It can also be useful to preach through a theme. The Bible is full of vital themes for the Christian life. I remember hearing a series of sermons on forgiveness. They were inspiring, practical and dealt with this hugely important subject at a time when many in the audience needed to hear about it. I have personally preached sermons on such themes as spiritual warfare, prayer and evangelism.

Preaching through a theme will enable you to deal with relevant issues which your church needs to be aware of. Recently in my own church we became aware of the need to encourage church members to participate more fully in the life and work of the church. We decided to preach a series of sermons on the Gifts of the Holy Spirit. The effect of this series meant that the members of the church not only realised that they each had gifts, but in many cases were also motivated to put their gifts to good use. The unanimous feeling among church members was that it had been a very worthwhile theme to cover.

Preaching through a Key Passage

There is value too in preaching through some of the key passages of the Bible. All of Scripture is inspired and profitable, but there are some passages which are particularly important and helpful, and these need to be emphasised. Again such a series can adapt to the needs of the church at any given time.

I once remember hearing a series of sermons on the Sermon on the Mount. This section of Matthew's Gospel is not only challenging, it also gives us a manifesto for Christian living. In it Jesus sums up what it means to follow him and the implications of joining the Christian counterculture. Such is the importance of this passage of Scripture that it deserves regular attention in the teaching programme of the local church.

There are many other key passages that merit inclusion in this list of great passages of the Bible. The creation accounts of Genesis chapters 1 to 3 are hugely important to modern Christians who are in danger of forgetting the sanctity of life (especially human life) and the importance of God's role as creator of all things. The great passage on faith (Hebrews 11) and the wonderful passage on love (1 Corinthians 13) are also worthy candidates. The Letters to the Seven Churches

(Revelation 1-3) are very helpful as is the chapter on the Ten Commandments (Exodus 20). Each of these key passages, and many others, would make an excellent series of sermons that would benefit any church.

Whether you are preaching through a book, a theme, the life of a biblical character or a great passage, remember always to make your sermon expository. The passage must be seen in it's context. The grammar, type of literature and historical background must be taken into consideration. You must also remember that your job is not so much to give an opinion on a particular issue, but to declare what God says and apply this to your audience.

Preaching the Whole Bible

It is also important to state that preachers have the responsibility to bring the whole of God's Word to their congregation. It is a sad fact that many a church preaching syllabus ignores a great deal of the Bible. I have frequently conducted surveys with my students to ascertain what bible books they have heard preached on in their church over the past few years. In almost every case they will have heard sermons on Genesis, the Psalms, Isaiah, Jonah, Daniel, John's Gospel, Romans, Galatians, Philippians and Revelation. But almost none of them have heard sermons on Leviticus, Esther, Ezekiel, Habbakkuk, Titus or Jude.

Whatever the reason, many preachers choose to ignore large chunks of the Bible, preferring to stick to a few favourite books. This is always a mistake. God has given us his Word so we can learn about him and his work. If we ignore any biblical book, we ignore part of God's message to us. It seems only reasonable that every church should cover the whole Bible in it's preaching programme. I know of some churches that systematically preach through the whole Bible every ten years. Such a feat takes courage, determination and a confidence in all of Scripture. It will, however, bear much fruit in the long run.

Courage, Humility and Consistency

Up until this point I have focussed on the mechanics of a preacher's job. But there is more to preaching than just the exposition of Scripture. Every good preacher not only needs the technical ability to understand and communicate Scripture, he also needs integrity to give his ministry credibility. No definition of a preacher's job would be complete without mentioning the personal qualities which this kind of ministry requires.

There are three qualities a preacher will need if his ministry is to be effective. The first of these is courage. Declaring God's Word has never be an easy business. Amos discovered this while preaching to the crowds at Bethel. He quickly found himself under attack from Amaziah (Amos 7:10-17). Today's preachers might not have to face the same vocal barrage, but opposition can nevertheless be real.

People don't always like the truth. Even Christians struggle to cope with truth when it confronts them. This is particularly the case when they are convicted by it. Sometimes this conviction leads to repentance, but sometimes not. Many preachers have found themselves under attack from people in their own church because of what they have said from the pulpit. No doubt some preachers have deserved criticism because they have said things in an offensive way or what they have said has simply been wrong. However, I know of many situations where godly preachers have correctly declared the Word of God in an appropriate way and as a result have been severely criticised.

It is easy to become discouraged as a preacher. The pulpit is a vulnerable and lonely place to be. Hard messages are always hard to preach, but they need to be heard. Proper preaching, which involves declaring what God is saying through his Word, is therefore something which requires great courage. Without courage and the willingness to preach the Bible honestly, without ducking difficult issues, a preacher will never be able to fulfil his obligations.

The second essential quality which all preachers need is humility. As well as the criticisms, there are the complements. I have found that most churches are appreciative of the preaching they receive. Many kind people have thanked me after a sermon and told me that they found what I said to be of help. This is all very nice, but such generous remarks can also flatter the ego and give the preacher a swollen head.

Preaching by its very nature is public and high profile. Preachers are often held in high esteem within their churches. In many churches the preacher(s) will have a great deal of influence, perhaps even power. None of this can be avoided and it is entirely in order that those who minister the Word of God are honoured (1 Tim.5:17). Better the honour than the criticism. But in order to handle this, preachers need to have their feet firmly on the ground and in particular they need to be humble.

There is nothing more objectionable than a preacher who is full of his own self importance. Pride in the pulpit is not only unpleasant, it destroys a ministry. It prevents us from being all that we could be for God. Preachers who are proud tend to focus their audience's attention on themselves rather than on Christ. In the long run this will leave the audience empty and suffering from spiritual malnutrition. Humility, on the other hand, enables a preacher to lead his audience to the person of Christ, and there they find spiritual strength.

The third essential quality of a good preacher is consistency in his personal life. The old adage says, 'you should always practise what you preach'. This is never more true than when it comes to those who preach the Word of God. James tells us that those who would teach will be judged more harshly (James 3:1). This is quite true. It is utter hypocrisy to demand a certain standard of conduct from the members of your church or any group of Christians if you are not prepared to live up to those standards yourself. Such hypocrisy is worthy of judgment indeed!

It is not that preachers are or can be perfect. None of us are paragons of virtue. Frankly it is impossible for any preacher to live a faultless life. After all we do have feet of clay. However, glaring inconsistencies in the life of a preacher will utterly destroy his credibility and consequently his ministry. If he does not endeavour to live up to what he preaches, one of two things will happen. Either his congregation will come to the conclusion that if the preacher himself cannot do it no one can, or they will simply ignore all that he says for he shows no evidence of it in his own life. Either way his sermons will be utterly ineffective.

This then is the job of the preacher: to declare God's word by giving his congregation an exposition of

Scripture. This is to be done with courage and humility and the preacher is not just to preach the Word of God, but live it also.

Summary:
- A preacher is not an entertainer.
- A preacher should not merely tell people what they want to hear, but challenge them.
- A preacher is not just a storyteller.
- Expository preaching is communicating a biblical message through a historical, grammatical and literary study of a passage in its context.
- Expository preaching can include whole books, characters, themes and sections.
- The whole Bible needs to be preached courageously, humbly and consistently.

Pause for Thought:
Reflect on your own journey towards a preaching ministry, and on your present situation. What influences shaped you and to what extent has your preaching been truly expository.

5

The Art of Reading the Bible

Having a desire to preach is one thing, being able to do so is quite another. God wishes to speak through the preacher to his church, but the preacher must first understand what God is saying. This brings us to the issue of bible study. Before we can preach from the Bible, we need to have a grasp of its content.

A book as ancient and varied as the Bible needs to be studied carefully. It is also vital that we apply principles of biblical interpretation to our study. Without interpreting what we read, the Bible will make little sense. The discipline of interpretation is known as hermeneutics. This word comes from the Greek *hermeneia* which means 'to explain, or to interpret'.

An Old Book

There are obvious reasons as to why applying hermeneutics to our bible study is essential to our understanding of the Bible. Firstly, there is a distance in time between different events described in the Bible as well as a distance in time between the completion of the Bible and the present day. The Bible itself spans centuries and about two thousand years have passed since the Bible was completed. The most recent situations mentioned in the Bible are therefore two thousand years old while others are thousands of years older.

The world my grandparents lived in seems very remote to me as it is very different from the one I now inhabit. When I watch period dramas set in the seventeenth century or read history books which cover the medieval period I am even more struck by the changes that have taken place in society over the centuries. The biblical world is more ancient still and therefore very much more different. This difference needs to be understood in order for the message of the Bible to be understood.

Different Culture

As well as time distance separating us from the events of the Bible, there are also huge cultural distances separating biblical times from the modern day. The world of the Bible knows nothing about information technology, cars, newspapers, industrial pollution or democratic forms of government. It is a world based around agriculture where landowners hold sway over the lives of the people who work on their farms. A world where travel is slow and dangerous and where neither medication nor education were taken for granted as they are in many countries today.

Different Language

There are also language differences separating us from the words of Scripture. Modern day English is very different from biblical Hebrew or Greek. Hebrew is Semitic in origin and paints vivid word pictures to compensate for the limitations of it's imprecise and sparse vocabulary. Biblical Greek does not recognise the chronological sentence structures which govern English. An understanding of how these languages work is therefore essential to understanding the content of biblical passages.

Who Needs Hermeneutics

For all of these reasons we need to apply our minds to interpreting the Bible. Unless we do so we will never understand what God is saying. We need to be able to differentiate between the voice of God in a passage and the voice of human culture. The Bible talks about polygamy, the evil of lending money and kissing fellow Christians. We need to be able to decide whether God wants us to be polygamous, to ban banking and to kiss every church member we meet, or whether these are cultural issues which are not binding. Only a proper system of hermeneutics will enable us to do this.

God has spoken, but he has chosen to do so within a specific cultural, linguistic and historical framework. The job of the interpreter is to find the principles which govern how Scripture works and then use those principles to determine how Scripture can be applied to a contemporary situation.

I will pick up on these specific issues in more detail in the next chapter, but in the meantime, I want to deal with some of the most basic issues of biblical study.

The Discipline of Reading

The very first thing we need to do in order to understand a passage of Scripture is to read it carefully. I have often had to correct myself for rushing into the preparation of a sermon without really getting to grips with the passage. Pressures of time and an inbuilt laziness will always be a problem, but time spent repeatedly reading a passage is never wasted. It is good not just to read the immediate passage that you are studying, but the whole book as well. Most books in the Bible can be read in less than an hour, and reading the whole book in one sitting will give you an idea of the thought flow that the author had in mind.

If I am preaching systematically through a bible book, I will read the whole book through at least twice, and then as I prepare each sermon I will read the relevant passage through again, usually several times. Different people pick up different amounts of information as they read. Personally, I need to read a passage through at least five or six times before it really sinks in. How you read is important. I find it helpful to read a passage a couple of times quickly just to get a general picture of what is being said. Then I read it a few more times, but more carefully and slowly.

Question the Text

As you read it is also good to ask yourself a few questions about the passage. Who are the principal characters (if any) in this passage? Why is it being written? What does it teach me about God? What does it teach me about myself? Is it warning me about anything? Is there a command that should be followed? Is there an example for me to imitate? In what ways does this passage encourage me? All your answers to these questions and your reflections should be written down.

I have invariably found that the more questions I ask of the text the more I discover its meaning, and in turn this enriches my preaching. A good preacher is like a good detective searching for clues. Find all the clues and the mystery behind the passage is solved.

As well as asking all the necessary questions, try to identify key words. These key words embody the meaning of the text and so are vital. As all Scripture is inspired by God, each word is there deliberately and is important. It is useful to write these key words down on a piece of paper so you can look at them further. You may also want to underline them in your Bible. Here is an example of the kind of key words I would pick out of a passage:

Consider it pure joy my brothers, whenever you face trials of many kinds because you know that the testing of your faith develops perseverance. Perseverance must finish its work so that you may be mature and complete, not lacking anything. If any of you lacks wisdom, he should ask of God, who gives generously to all without finding fault, and it will be given to him. But when he asks, he must believe and not doubt, because he who doubts is like a wave of the sea, blown and tossed by the wind. This man should not think he will receive anything from the Lord; he is a double-minded man, unstable in all he does.

As you pick out these words, make a mental note as to whether they are verbs, adjectives, adverbs or nouns. This is basic grammar, but if precision is what you are looking for, then it is very important to your understanding of the passage. The verbs will tell you what is being done, the adverbs will fill in the details of the action, the nouns will tell you what people, places or things are involved, and the adjectives will describe those people, places or things. It is also good to look for the prepositions. These are words like *on*, *at*, *in* and *after* which express the relationship between a noun and the other words in the sentence.

When you think about the individual words within a passage and their relationship with each other, you begin to see more clearly exactly what is being said.

Looking at the Context

After thinking about the passage itself, it is important to think about the wider context. Always think in paragraphs and sections, never be tempted to take any one verse out of context. This could lead to all kinds of problems. For example, if you were to read Habakkuk 1:5 by itself where God says, 'I am raising up the Babylonians', and you did not look at the wider context, you could get the distinct impression that the evil Babylonians are enjoying God's favour and they are being blessed by God. The context, however, tells a different story.

Although the chapter divisions in the Bible are not part of the original text, they can be a useful guide, but don't adhere too slavishly to them. Think about the whole chapter and ask yourself in what way the passage you are thinking about relates to the whole chapter.

You will also need to think about the book as a whole. Where does this passage come in relation to the whole book and how does it contribute to the message of the book? At what point does it come in the argument and why? Remember that Paul never intended the churches just to read sections of his letters in isolation. Neither did any of the other biblical writers intend for us to look at just one little part of their work. The whole context is therefore of great importance.

Even at this point you cannot stop. You need to compare what you have learned in this passage with the other writings by the same author (if there are any), and then with the whole Testament, and the whole Bible. The Bible has sixty-six different books written by many different authors, but it is one complete message. There will be no contradiction between your passage and any other in the Bible, but there will be many other passages that will shed light on the passage that you are studying.

These other passages will give balance to your understanding. Bear in mind also that each biblical author will have his own distinct emphasis. The book of Romans deals with the issue of faith in a different way to the book of James. Both are inspired and therefore your understanding of the issue of faith will be enriched by reading both what James and Paul have to say about it.

All of this sounds like a great deal of hard work. It is hard work! But time must be invested in reading and study if a passage is to be understood.

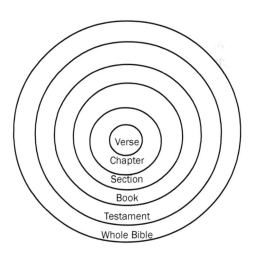

Summary:
- The Bible is an old book with a culture and language different from our own. Interpretation is therefore essential.
- The text needs to be read thoroughly and questioned.
- It is vital to look at the wider context of any passage.

Pause for Thought:
To what extent do you read Scripture carefully, questioning it and thinking about its cultural background? Endeavour to develop this habit, whenever you read Scripture, so that it becomes a habit.

6

Language, History and Culture

Having thoroughly read the passage, the time has now come to do some detailed study. In short, you need to look at the language, history and culture behind the passage. This process begins by giving more attention to those key words that you noted down. Time needs to be spent thinking about their meaning, and you need to ask yourself why that particular word was used in this way. It will be important at this stage to use some resources in your study.

In dealing with specific words and phrases it is important to be reminded that the languages of the Bible are very different to contemporary English. Indeed, languages in general will differ from each other in their ability to communicate precise ideas as well as having their own vocabulary and internal rules. The difference is amplified when dealing with the biblical languages as they are so ancient, and in the case of Hebrew because it is Semitic rather than European.

Key Words

As you begin to look at the key words you have noted, there are a number of issues that you will need to be aware of. Firstly, most words have a range of meanings. Some refer to this as a 'field of meaning' (or even a semantic field). Take the English word 'hand' as an example. This word will change its meaning depending on the context in which it is found. If I told you that I would like to 'shake your hand', that would communicate a different message to you than if I told you that I would like to 'give you a hand'. The first use refers to a part of the body and the second to the action of helping you. If we had an audience I might ask them to 'give you a big hand'. Once again, although the same word is being used, the meaning is different.

When it comes to many biblical words, there is also a range of meanings and this is determined, for the most part, by the context. It is important, therefore, to locate the precise meaning of the word within its context. If you fail to do this, you may misinterpret the passage.

To further complicate matters you need to bear in mind that words overlap. The same word can refer to two distinct areas of life. Take a word like 'runner', for instance. It can be linked with the world of athletics to describe someone who takes part in a race. But it can also be linked with the world of horticulture to describe a twining plant. Again the same word, but the meaning exists in at least two different worlds. Within each world there will be other words that have the same basic meaning, but with slightly different variations. For example the word 'runner', when used in the world of athletics, has the same basic meaning as 'jogger' or 'sprinter'. The difference between these words is that sprinter and jogger refer to specific types of running. By seeing the whereabouts of a word in a field of meaning, you can get a more precise definition of what that word actually means.

If we were to take the word 'peace' (the Greek word for peace is *eirene*) as an example, we would notice that this word belongs to two different semantic fields.[1] On the one hand, it can refer to the absence of trouble and therefore share meanings with other words within that semantic field. On the other, it can refer to a state of mind in which the person is free of anxiety. So when we come across this word 'peace' in the Bible (Rom.12:18 ; Phil.4:7) we need to make up our minds as to which of these semantic fields we should opt for. Then we discover whereabouts in the semantic field it belongs.

A second thing that you will have to bear in mind is that words change their meaning over a period of time. Take the word 'gay' as an example. In Victorian England it would not have been an insult to describe someone as 'gay', on the contrary it would suggest a happy, lighthearted and carefree personality. To use the word today, however, is a different matter as it now refers to a person's sexual orientation. The same is true of the word 'fantastic'. If you told your girlfriend that she looked fantastic she would be delighted. Back in Victorian times, however, you may well get a slap across the face as the word then meant grotesque or freakish.

When it comes to biblical vocabulary, the same applies. There are some words which have changed their meaning over time, so when they are found in the biblical text, the meaning that was intended at the time of writing needs to be found. One example for this is the word *'martus'* which in Revelation 2:13 is translated 'witness'. The word 'martus' began its career referring to someone who gave evidence, possibly in a court of law. It went on to refer to a person who gave witness to their beliefs. Later it referred to a person who witnessed to their faith even under threat, and finally to someone who was willing to die for their cause, thus becoming a martyr.[2] If an interpreter were to translate the word *'martus'* in Revelation 2:13 as martyr, he would most likely be wrong.[3] Even though Antipas did die for his faith, the word *'martus'* probably did not refer to martyrdom at this stage, but rather to someone who witnessed to their faith even under pressure.

A third thing to bear in mind is that words can have meanings other than the most obvious. The extra meaning may be figurative, and the interpreter will need to decide if the word should be interpreted literally or in a figurative way. I can remember on one occasion referring to one of my teachers as a 'battle-axe'. Clearly on that occasion the use of the word was not literal. She was not a weapon of war. She did, however, have the kind of personality which made the figurative use of the word appropriate.

Paul does exactly this as he attacks the Jews in Philippians 3:2 by describing them as 'dogs'. In the ancient world dogs were rarely treated as household pets. If they were used domestically, it was as guard dogs. Often dogs wandered the streets as scavengers, eating filth and rubbish. It was this uncleanness that Paul was hinting at as he attacked these Jews who saw themselves as being a cut above the rest.[4]

Bearing all these issues in mind, how do we go about a study of the key words that we have identified? The process is twofold. First you need to determine what the range of meaning of that word was at the time when the author penned it. You are asking the question, what could this word possibly have meant as the writer was putting pen to paper? Your intention is to get as much information as possible about the use of vocabulary at that time.

In order to help you determine this you will need to use a lexicon. It will tell you the possible range of meanings throughout a given period of history. They do this by utilising information culled from a variety of literary sources within that time frame. Their sources include Scripture but also a wider body of literature. In addition to a lexicon you will find bible dictionaries, bible encyclopaedias and theological dictionaries an invaluable source of information. This may involve a lot of work, but the benefits of discovering the meanings of the word in question far outweigh the sacrifice of time and energy.

Once you have found all the possible meanings for the word, the second step is to discover which meaning best fits the passage. This is done by looking at the context. It may well be that the general subject matter of the passage strongly and obviously suggests one of the meanings you have discovered. If that is the case, you have easily arrived at the conclusion. If not, you may well need to look for further clues in order to determine the meaning. These clues may involve looking at how the same writer uses the same word in other passages or even how other writers dealing with the same subject use that kind of vocabulary.

Grammar and Structure

Having done all this, you now need to discover how the word you are looking at fits into the overall structure of the sentence. This takes you into the discipline of grammar and structure. There are two aspects to grammar, morphology and syntax.[5] Morphology is about the form of a word. In English if you add the letter *s* to the end of a word it becomes plural. Thus *car* becomes *cars*. In Hebrew, letters are also added to the end of words to make them plural. Greek is slightly different in that it adds letters at the end of words, but also links this with endings that denote if the word is nominative, genitive or dative.

Syntax, on the other hand, describes the grammatical arrangement of words and their relationship to each other. In English, word order determines the relationship between words in a sentence. If I say that 'Billy stabbed Mark and Paul', Billy is clearly the culprit, with Mark and Paul being the victims. If, on the other hand, I say that 'Paul stabbed Mark and Billy', then Paul becomes the culprit. In Greek and Hebrew, word order is not as important, but both languages do demonstrate the relationship words have with each other.

Clearly it is important to understand both the form of the words you are studying and how they relate to the other words in the sentence. This will add to your understanding of the passage as a whole and enable you to make a more accurate interpretation. Obviously a knowledge of Hebrew and Greek will help you in this process. If you do not have any knowledge of these languages you will be at a slight disadvantage. But however little or much you know of the original languages, a good commentary will be of enormous help. You will, however, need one which is sufficiently detailed that it deals with these linguistic technicalities.

History and Culture

Now that you know the meanings of key words in the text and understand their relationship to the sentences in which they appear, it is time to think of their historical and cultural location.

Writing cannot be done in a vacuum. We all come from a background that influences the way we see the world. I grew up in Northern Ireland which for many years has been a divided community. The recent history of the country has been peppered with many unforgettable events such as terrorist bombs, shootings, hunger strikes and political posturing. One of the things I used to do when some of these events took place was to read a variety of newspapers which came from both traditions within the country. Sometimes when reading two different newspapers you might think that they were describing entirely unconnected events as their reporting of the issues was so different. In one newspaper a particular politician would be treated like some kind of hero, while in another, he was seen as a rogue and a trouble-maker.

If the world of 'objective reporting' is so tainted with the culture and history of the writer, all other kinds of literature will be as well. This, of course, includes the Bible. In much the same way as a newspaper needs to be interpreted in the light of its historical and cultural situation, so does the Bible. The issue is, however, more complex than this. To begin with, it is entirely possible for a newspaper to lie, or to communicate a message that is irrelevant and unimportant. The Bible, on the other hand, is the Word of God and therefore of utmost importance. It still requires interpretation but the stakes are higher as the meaning is crucial.

What is more, we are eavesdropping on the biblical text. As you read a newspaper you are aware that you are the intended recipient of the message. The journalist, who shares your culture and lives in the same era as you, is writing directly to you. Not so with the Bible. As we read we are listening in to a communication between people who lived over two thousand years ago in a different era and from a completely different culture. Their setting is a world away from ours. The mindset of the author will also be different. He will not think in the same way as you do and his expressions will be different from yours.

All of this makes interpretation very much more difficult as you are trying to discover what a particular verse or biblical statement meant to the person who wrote it. What did Amos mean when he referred to the Israelite women as 'cows of Bashan' (Amos 4:1)? And what did Jesus mean when he referred to the Pharisees as 'whitewashed tombs' (Mtt.23:27)? Clearly an understanding of the mindset of the biblical writers is crucial.

Transporting the Text

Of course, going back into the world of the biblical author is only half the job. You then have to bring the meaning back to the present day, otherwise people living now will have no idea what the message is all about. This process is sometimes referred to as context-ualization.[6] It is a bit like using a time machine and going back centuries to the world of the Bible, picking up a meaning, and then returning to the present day in the time machine so that meaning can be grasped by your contemporaries.

I spent my early childhood in Ethiopia where people (speaking a different language) used expressions that would be alien to anyone from the United Kingdom. One expression that Ethiopians used was *te fitfit achu feet*, which literally reads 'not the food but the face'. To a British person this is meaningless but to an Ethiopian it is full of meaning. For them it says that when a person goes to the house of a friend, the quality of food is not the thing that makes him feel welcome, but the smiling face and warmth of his host. I could not use this expression in conversation with my friends in this country, even if I translated it. In order for them to understand the significance of what I am saying I need to contextualise the sentiment of the expression, transporting it into contemporary English parlance.

Contextualization

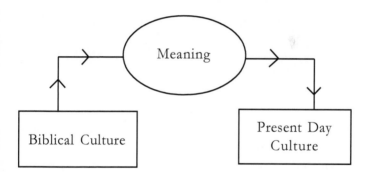

In much the same way, we need to transport the biblical meaning into our modern society by putting it into an intelligible form. Without doing so the meaning of the text will remain disguised and we will miss the point of what is being said.

Steps to Understanding
How do we go about this process of understanding the historical context of a passage and making it intelligible to modern hearers? The key is to look at the background and build up a picture of the times in which the biblical events took place.

This process begins by looking at the general background of the book as a whole. Again it is important to ask all kinds of questions. Who was the author? Where did he come from? When did he write this book? What were the circumstances of his life when he wrote it? What was his purpose in writing the book? Who comprised his original audience? As each of these questions is answered, a basic picture begins to emerge of the setting.

You may also wish to ask questions about what was happening in the wider world at the time of writing. Who was the world superpower at that time? Was Israel under the domination of an empire, and if so which one? How did the wider political scene impact upon life in Israel? What was it like to be a devoted follower of God, or a Christian at this time?

Many of these questions will be answered within the text itself, however, it will be essential to make use of the extensive range of study material which is available to us. For example, you will find an Old Testament Survey or New Testament Survey to be of great help. You will also benefit from books that describe the history of the Old and New Testaments. Good commentaries will again come in useful, particularly in their introductory studies, and Bible dictionaries will also pay dividends. There is an extensive range of excellent books which look at the background to many of the biblical events, peoples and places. Read all you can and get as much information as you can.

Having looked at the background of the book, you will then need to look in more detail at the background of the specific passage you are studying. Again you need to ask more questions, but this time you are trying to discover what the writer meant by what he wrote. In other words, in the light of the circumstances in which the author was writing, what is the most likely interpretation of the passage?

Depending on the content of the passage, you may have to ask some very specific questions. For example, what were the social customs that governed the author's life and environment? What were the roles of men, women and children in his society? How was worship typically conducted in that day? What kind of theology or religious ideas confronted the author? What were the economic structures of the day? What were the prevailing world views of the day?

Once again the books mentioned above will be helpful. Your goal is to look at all the available evidence and construct a picture within which you can fit the passage so that it makes sense.

Some years ago I visited the Natural History Museum. It was a wonderful day out, but the most memorable feature of the museum was a huge dinosaur skeleton which towered over all the visitors. Our guide for the day told us that the skeleton was not found buried in one piece. Indeed not all of the bones were authentic, many had been constructed just for the exhibit. What had happened was that palaeontologists working on the project had unearthed some bones from different sights and had begun to piece them together as they gathered data on that particular dinosaur from their study. Their information had been so well gathered that they were able to manufacture some bones so as to present a completed dinosaur skeleton to the museum.

The work of constructing meaning from a biblical text is similar. The more background information you can get, the more accurately you will understand the passage and the better equipped you will be to interpret it correctly.

Summary:

- Words need to be studied carefully as they can be used in different ways, they overlap, and their meanings change over time.
- The grammar and structure of a sentence can alter its meaning.
- Any given passage needs to be read within its cultural and historical context.
- We need to take the meaning of a passage and transport that meaning into our contemporary setting.

Pause for Thought:

The work of interpreting a passage requires diligence and attention to detail. For this reason preachers are often put off by the effort required, and instead feed their congregation on a poor diet of sermons devoid of solid and meaningful content. We need to recognise that we are dealing with God=s word which is infinitely precious. The investment of time and energy is therefore worthwhile.

Understanding Genre

Even when you have understood the language used in a particular passage of Scripture and have built up a picture of the historical and cultural context in which that passage emerges, your job is still not complete. There remains one last vital stage in the process of correctly interpreting Scripture. I refer to the issue of understanding the type of literature used in any given passage.

The Bible is a fascinating and complex book in which we find many different types of literature, or genre. Common sense will tell you that you would not read the poems of Wilfred Owen in the same way as you read your daily newspaper. Neither would you treat a chemistry textbook in the same way as you would a science fiction novel. These different genre need to be understood in the light of the laws that govern them. They can only be understood if these laws are applied.

The same principles must apply to our reading and study of the Bible. In the Bible we find a variety of literary genre including narrative, poetry, prophetic, wisdom, gospel, epistle and apocalyptic. Only when we correctly understand the inner workings of these genre can we hope to understand their meaning.

Narrative
The first type of literature we need to consider is narrative. Narrative is the most common genre found

within the Bible.[1] In the Old Testament alone narrative occupies approximately 40 per cent of the text. Narrative could be defined as 'a spoken or written account of connected events in order of happening'.[2] In other words, this form of literature deals with a storyline and describes the experiences which the people in that storyline had. It enables the reader to take part in what is happening and sense the occasion.

That being the case, if the reader really wants to get the most from a section of narrative, he needs to try and visualise it for himself. To a degree this involves using a certain amount of imagination. But just as you might enjoy a good novel if you actually picture yourself in the shoes of one of the characters, or if you imagine that you are actually at the scene of an event that you are reading, so biblical narrative encourages us to enter into the story. By doing so we will not only enjoy the story more, we will understand it much better.

The Characters

But how do stories work? In what way are we meant to read and understand them? Firstly, we need to recognise that at the centre of every story there are the people involved. These characters will be the main attraction. We learn about them in a variety of ways. The writer may give us a description of a particular character (1 Sam.2:13). The characters themselves may tell us what they are like (Gen.39:8,9). We can also learn a great deal about the character from what they say (1 Kg.3:7-9). Their actions might portray a great deal about the kind of people they are (Ezra 7:10). We can also learn about them from the way others relate to them in the story (Gen.31:31).

Once all this information has been put together it gives us a useful profile of the people within the story. This is the first stage and the basic foundation block for understanding what the story is about.

The Plot

The second feature of a story is the plot itself. I have often told my students that a story cannot be a story unless it is a story. This is quite true. There will be a storyline woven throughout the text of a narrative. Sometimes it will be complex and intriguing, other times fairly uneventful, but always important.

A prominent feature in much of biblical narrative is the struggle that some of the biblical characters have as they go through life. David faced struggles in his conflicts with Goliath, King Saul and the Philistines. Joseph faced struggles in his relationship with his brothers and in the false accusations made against him by Potiphar's wife. It is important not only to follow the storyline but also to observe in detail how these struggles arise and are subsequently solved.

Sometimes there can be more than one storyline running side by side. There will be some connection between these yet this is not necessarily apparent at the beginning of the stories. The life of Abraham is a good example of this. On the one hand there is an account of a man who is called by God to leave his home and go to the place where God would call him. On the other, there is the story of a man who longs for a son but is unable to father one. Ultimately there is a connection, but until these threads are brought together, the different storylines have their own lives and purpose in the narrative.

The Setting

The third feature that we need to note in any story is the setting. The stories that we find in biblical narrative are actual historical events. There is nothing fictitious about them. They are real accounts of God's dealings with men. That being the case, these are stories that take place in real geographical and physical settings at an actual time in history. Understanding the story, therefore, requires a little background information and research to obtain an accurate idea of the world in which the story occurs.

Once you get a picture of the setting of a story, it becomes vivid and alive. If you can grasp the awful dank and dreary setting of the prison cell in Acts 16, then the story of the imprisonment of Paul and his companions in Philippi becomes all too real. Or if you can imagine how terrifying it must have been to look across a ravine and see a giant challenging anyone to a representative battle then you have some concept of how David must have felt as he went to face Goliath. Once the setting is comprehended and the characters and storyline are understood, then the meaning of the narrative can be explored.

Tips on Preaching from Narrative

How is narrative to be interpreted? What lessons are we to learn from this type of literature? And specifically, how are we to preach narrative passages?

As narratives are stories, they will need to be told as stories. This will involve a dramatic presentation and the use of imagination. A good storyteller knows the background of the story, the main characters and is able to create the atmosphere in which the story becomes compelling. Part of the presentation will involve answering questions necessary for an understanding of the passage. Who are the main people involved? Why are they behaving as they are? What is the main purpose of the story? The answer to each of these questions will be an essential part of the sermon.

As we approach narrative, we need to bear in mind that as God revealed himself and his will to us, he did not do so using only a series of statements and demands. Indeed there are relatively few direct statements about what God is like and even fewer specific demands. He did, however, frequently reveal himself by inference. In other words, as we read a biblical passage there are clear principles implicit in the storyline from which we can learn about God and his will.

Never is this more so than in narrative passages. As we read about people and events in these narrative passages, we draw lessons for our lives. Of course much of our general learning in life is done this way. A child will learn about the kind of people his parents are by observing how they behave. He will also learn how to behave by how they react to whatever he does. If he does something positive, they will tell him so and give him a hug (or a sweet). If he is naughty he will end up with a sore bottom. In much the same way we can learn from narrative by observation.

When a narrative is preached there are three ways of drawing lessons or applications for the audience. Firstly, we can learn from the good or bad examples of the characters involved. If I were preaching on the narrative of David's battle with Goliath, I would point out that this was a young man who was concerned to defend the honour of God and was not afraid to do battle with the giant because of his trust in God (1 Sam.16:26). The application would encourage the audience to be concerned for God's honour in their lives and to live courageously, knowing that God was with them.

Secondly, we can learn lessons from the way in which God dealt with people in the narrative. In the story of Lot's wife, she turned back to look at the cities that were being destroyed (Gen.19:26). As a consequence she was turned into a pillar of salt. This passage teaches the seriousness of disobedience and the danger of not making a clean break with our sinful past.

Thirdly, we can learn lessons from what people in the passage discovered about their actions. In the story of Samson, the hero led an irresponsible life and the consequences came back to haunt him. Ultimately it took an action from God to vindicate him and make his life useful again. Samson's story teaches us that our lifestyle has an impact on our usefulness to God and that we can end up wasting our lives engaging in futile pursuits.

As these lessons emerge from the narrative, they can be preached with confidence, for these biblical stories contain lessons by inference which are just as powerful a guide as direct commands.

Poetry

Another important genre in the Bible is that of poetry. Some of the biblical books are entirely poetry, such as the Psalms, Song of Solomon, Proverbs and Lamentations. Others, such as Job, Ecclesiastes, Isaiah, Hosea and Joel, contain substantial sections of poetry. Some scholars have even argued that there is no book in the Bible that does not require the reader to have some knowledge of how to interpret poetry.[3] Though biblical poetry is unique within the world of poetry in that it is inspired and authoritative, it is not the only poetry to come from the ancient Near East. Indeed Israel benefited from a well-developed literary tradition within the ancient Near East, some of which dated all the way back to 3,200 BC.[4]

Parallelism

When we think of biblical poetry we must not confuse it with our modern English poetry. English poetry is based on rhyme so that the final words in a line sound similar. Hebrew poetry, though it does sometimes make some use of sounds, is much more dependent on parallelism. Parallelism is a literary device that reinforces or develops an idea by repeating it in a slightly different way in the succeeding line or lines.[5] It brings a sharper focus on the message being communicated.

Some scholars have argued that there are just three different types of parallelism.[6] This, however, is certainly an underestimation.[7] Each type of parallelism is trying to achieve a particular effect. The most common of these is called *Synonymous parallelism*. This is the repetition of the same thought using closely related but slightly differing sets of words. A good example of this is found in Psalm 103:10:

He does not treat us as our sins deserve
or repay us according to our iniquities.

Another type is *Antithetic parallelism*. This type of parallelism functions in much the same way as does synonymous parallelism. It communicates the same idea in a different way in the second line, but this time it does it by using words that are opposite of the first words expressed. This usage of opposites is known as using antonyms. Tall is the opposite (or antonym) of short. Dark the opposite of light. By using an opposite set of words, the writer can emphasise his point by making this contrast. An example of this type of parallelism is found in Psalm 37:21:

> The wicked borrow and do not repay,
> but the righteous give generously.

There is also *climactic parallelism*. That is a repetitious parallelism which brings the reader to a crescendo by emphasising a point in slightly different ways and developing the idea. Usually several lines or phrases are used in this type of parallelism. If read properly, the reader will feel a growing sense of excitement with each line. An example of this is found in Psalm 29:1:

> Ascribe to the Lord, O mighty ones
> ascribe to the Lord glory and strength.
> Ascribe to the Lord glory due to his name;
> worship the Lord in the splendour of his holiness.

Then there are *emblematic parallelisms*. These add to the richness of a thought by using an analogy. Something is compared to another thing from a completely different sphere of life. For example, God might be compared to a rock. This analogy enables the reader to see the richness of the person or thing that the writer is referring to, by taking note of the characteristics of the thing to which the subject is being compared. Here are a couple of examples taken from Psalm 42:1 and Psalm 72:6:

As the deer pants for streams of water,
so my soul pants for you, O God.

He will be like rain falling on a mown field,
like showers watering the earth.

There are also *pivot parallelisms* in Hebrew poetry. In this case the pivot is a word which links both phrases in a parallelism. Some translations obscure these pivot words so they are difficult to identify. In the original Hebrew, however, they can be clearly seen. An example of this can be seen in Psalm 98:2 with 'to the nations' being the pivotal word.

The Lord has made his salvation known
to the nations and revealed his righteousness.

Finally there is a *chiasm*. In a chiasm an idea is put forward and is followed by two more ideas which relate to each other. Then there is a fourth idea which relates to the first one. A wellknown example of a chiasm is found in Psalm 1:1:

Blessed is the man who does not walk in the council
of the wicked or in the way of sinners stand.

This type of parallelism can best be demonstrated by using the letter X. In the case of the example we have mentioned, diagrammatically the psalm would look like this:

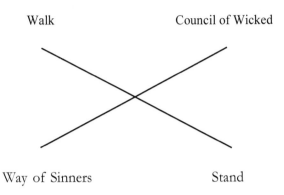

Walk   Council of Wicked

Way of Sinners   Stand

It is important when reading the psalms to pick out the parallelisms. Not every verse of poetry contains parallelisms. Many do not, but those that do contain them for a purpose and therefore they must be taken seriously. They are an integral part of the poetry and therefore will help us to identify its meaning. As you read these parallelisms you need to identify the way in which the writer has changed the phrases in order to create a parallelism. That will reveal to you his emphasis and thought flow and will prove vital for interpreting the poetry.

Imagery

In addition to parallelism, biblical poetry also has rich imagery. This imagery not only makes the poetry interesting by bringing it to life, it is also highly instructive. By paying attention to the images, we can learn a great deal about the writer's feelings towards a particular subject. In one sense the poet is an artist who paints pictures for us using words so that we can visualise his thoughts.

There are two types of imagery, similes and metaphors.[8] A simile is where two things are being compared to each other using the words 'like' or 'as'. If I were feeling romantic I could say that my wife is 'like a rose in full bloom'. In this way I compare her to a flower that has reached the height of its beauty.

A metaphor also compares two things but does so in a much more overt way. The words 'like' or 'as' are not used. If I were describing my wife using a metaphor I would say 'she is a rose in full bloom'. The metaphor evokes an even stronger response from the reader.

Metaphors and similes are very common in biblical poetry, particularly in relation to God. The Psalmist, for example, describes God as a rock, a fortress and a good shepherd.

Types of Psalms
One final thing that needs to be said about biblical poetry, is that it comes in different forms or types.[9] Some poetry is in the form of a hymn in which people are enthusiastically called upon to worship God. But there is also the lament in which the writer is crying out in distress. Then there are thanksgiving poems and poems of confidence in which the writer is either expressing thanks to God for his goodness, or recognising reasons why God can be trusted. There are remembrance poems which recall God's goodness to Israel in the past and wisdom poems where different ways of living are contrasted and the results described. Again the type of poem needs to be considered as it will reveal the mind-set of the writer and lead to a proper interpretation of the poetry.

Tips on Preaching from Poetry

We now need to think about how we preach poetic material. The first thing a preacher will need to do is to think about the experience that lies behind the passage of poetry. If you take some of the psalms as an example, you will often be able to identify the situation which prompted the writer to pen that particular psalm. Psalm 51 is an excellent example. This was written after David committed the sin of adultery with Bathsheba and then covered it up by having her husband killed. This psalm is profoundly moving and it expresses the deep-seated guilt that brought David to a point of confession and repentance. Discovering the experience enables the preacher to see why the psalm was written and that gives the backdrop to the sermon. A sermon on Psalm 51 would describe how a Christian must approach God after sinning.

A second step would be to identify any structure within a poem and use that for the structure of the sermon. Even at a first glance it is possible to see that many biblical poems are made up of stanzas. These help to break up the poem so that the reader can see where it is going. Take Psalm 1 as an example. The first three verses relate to those who follow God while the next three describe those who are wicked and do not. In each section the writer deals with the consequences of each respective lifestyle. In a sermon on Psalm 1, I would begin by describing the consequences of following God and would conclude by describing the fate of those who do not. In this case the structure of the psalm would indicate the necessary structure of the sermon.

Another pointer would be to identify any difficulty which the writer may be facing and then see how this difficulty is solved. Your sermon could question whether or not the writer's problems were self-inflicted and in what way he found help in God. In Psalm 3, for example, David found himself surrounded by many enemies. He dealt with this issue by realising that God was his shield and would protect him no matter what the difficulty.[10] A sermon on Psalm 3 would deal with the issue of discovering God's help in the midst of difficult situations.

One last thing that needs to be mentioned is that a bridge needs to be built between the experiences of the biblical characters and that of the contemporary audience. Your audience may not have found themselves embroiled in the sins of adultery and murder as David did, but there are many sins that we commit which put a strain on our relationship with God and require the kind of repentance that is described in Psalm 51. The link needs to be discovered so that the biblical poems can have a direct application in the lives of the audience.

Prophecy

Another common biblical genre is that of prophecy. In the Old Testament, God sent men to bring his word to the people when they had fallen away from their faith. The words and writings of these men form the prophetic literature of the Bible. These men lived in the same cultural context as their contemporaries, and they spoke in a language that their audience could understand, but their messages were revelations direct from God.[11]

Biblical prophecy does have a predictive element in that future events are foretold, but this is not always or even usually the case. Much of biblical prophecy addresses the situation at the time when the prophets spoke. They were speaking directly into a given situation.

Within the genre of prophecy there are a number of different types of prophetic literature.[12] The most common type is the *prophecy of disaster*. These were delivered to individuals in some instances, but to whole nations in others. The prophets brought a message to people who were sinning and it contained a threat of immanent disaster. The prophecy would contain a description of what the sins of the people were and often graphic language would be used to communicate the severity of the judgment. Jeremiah 28:12-14 is one typical example.

Another way of announcing doom was in the form of a *woe speech*. These are easy to identify as they begin with the phrase 'woe to you'. Again the sins of those who were being addressed are detailed. There is also a prediction of what will happen to these wicked people because of their sinfulness. A good example of a woe speech is in Amos 5:18-27.

Doom is also pronounced in the form of a *funeral dirge*. This type of prophecy was usually directed towards Israel and she was pictured as a corpse awaiting burial. Again the purpose is to pass on judgment to the nation. Once a person is dead there is little the mourners can do except lament the departure of their loved one. In much the same way the funeral dirge in prophetic literature emphasises the perilous condition of the nation and the certainty of divine judgment. Amos 5:1-3 is an example of a funeral dirge.

One of the most interesting forms of prophetic literature is that of the *prophetic lawsuit*. Here the prophet re-enacts a trial with Israel in the dock. Witnesses are called upon to give testimony against Israel, the nation has been summoned to the trial, and is duly indicted as a result of the charges. Often these prophecies make reference to the covenant between God and his people. The implication is clear. God has kept his side of the agreement, but Israel has failed. Therefore the judge must pass sentence on the nation. A typical lawsuit can be found in Hosea 4:1-3.

Not all prophecies were negative in content. Some were a clarion call to the nation to serve God faithfully while others predicted salvation and hope. The *prophetic hymns* are an example of prophecies which called on the nation to follow God. They exalted God and were an expression of thankfulness for all that God had done for the nation (Isa.42:10-13). Salvation was predicted in *salvation prophecies*. Here the prophets assured both individuals and nations that God would act for their benefit (Amos 9:11-15).

It is important to understand how biblical prophecies which are predictive in nature are fulfilled. In many cases biblical prophecies were literally fulfilled in precisely the manner in which the prophecy described. At other times, however, the prophecies were fulfilled figuratively. There were occasions when prophecies were fulfilled both literally and spiritually. In some cases there have even been multiple fulfilments. Take for example Daniel's prophecy dealing with the 'abomination of desolation' (Dan.9:27 ; 11:31 ; 12:11). It was first fulfilled when Antiochus Epiphanes made the Jews sacrifice pigs within the Holy of Holies in the Temple in 167BC. It was then fulfilled again at the destruction of Jerusalem and, according to some scholars, it will be fulfilled a third time in accordance with Mark 13:14.[13]

Tips on Preaching from the Prophets

How are the prophetic books and writings to be preached? What do we need to be aware of when we prepare sermons based on prophetic texts? The first thing to note is the vocabulary that the prophet employs. In observing the vocabulary, we must include proper nouns, for example Elam, Media, Babylon and Arabia (mentioned in Isaiah 21). We must not presume that these places are the same as those found on a modern atlas. The term Arabia, for example, is used of different places and these do not necessarily correspond to the modern nation of Arabia.[14]

It is also very important to discover the circumstances in which the prophet ministered. If he was speaking God's message into a particular situation, then it is unlikely that we will fully appreciate the meaning of his prophecy unless we understand that particular situation. This investigation must be methodical and systematic. You need to discover how the people mentioned were living, in what ways they were falling short of God's standards and any good or bad points that the prophet makes about them. This background information will enable you to see the relevance of the prophetic message and the current situations in which the message can be applied today.

When preaching though prophetic literature it is important also to pay close attention to the symbolisms which the prophets use. In the same way that poetry is brought to life and made more descriptive through imagery, so prophetic literature is made more powerful by the use of symbolism. Jeremiah uses the symbol of a potter to demonstrate that God wants his people to be malleable and willing to be moulded by a divine hand

(Jer.18:4). Amos uses the symbolism of a lion, a bear and a snake to demonstrate the inevitability of God's judgment (Amos 5:19). Ezekiel uses the symbolism of eating books to show that he was bringing God's message to the people (Ezek.3:1-3). These symbols will be key points in the sermon as they are the highlight of what the prophet is saying.

You must also look out for the reasons stated in the text for the judgment which is about to be dished out. This will also be a key factor in the interpretation. In Haggai the people were being judged because they were living in comfort while the Temple was in ruins (Haggai 1:4). In Habakkuk, judgment was immanent because the people were living unholy lives (Hab.1:3,4). These explanations will help to make the judgment understandable and will provide you with principles for living which can be applied to the audience.

Wisdom

Wisdom literature is possibly the most fascinating, and certainly the most philosophical genre in Scripture. It does not contain the kind of blunt commands as seen in the Ten Commandments (Ex.20) or the decisive voice of prophecy stating, 'Thus saith the Lord'. Rather it contains the cool and thoughtful comments of a wise teacher, struggling with difficult questions and urging us to think long and hard about life.[15]

The great benefit of wisdom literature is that it goes further and deeper into the recesses of our minds, even though it ultimately leaves many questions unanswered.[16] Though the wisdom books of the Old Testament are part of Scripture, they are not unique in the world of wisdom literature as many of the ancient peoples had their wisdom tradition. But within the biblical wisdom books, God has revealed divine truth through this medium so that we can ponder the 'deeper truths' of life from a Christian perspective.

Job, Proverbs and Ecclesiastes are very different books, even though they all come under the umbrella of wisdom writings. Job, for example, deals with the basic issue of suffering and does so by focussing on the specific sufferings of one man, Job himself. Despite his godliness he suffers physically, emotionally, mentally and spiritually. The book is structured around Job's conversations with his 'friends' who offer advice that is neither helpful nor theologically correct. Job could be described as a theodicy, that is a justification of God's work in the world.[17]

The book of Proverbs is quite different, dealing with the general issue of wisdom applied to everyday life. Longman and Dillard note that in Proverbs there are 'no references to the great acts of redemption or to the covenant, and there is very little explicit talk about God'.[18] The first part of the book (chapters 1-9) contain extended wisdom discourses while the second part (chapters 10-31) comprises a series of short pithy sayings which take the form of proverbs. There is undoubtedly a connection between these parts. Chapters 1-9 give us the principles of wisdom and this establishes the groundwork which makes the rest of the book, which deals with the outworking of these principles, meaningful.

Ecclesiastes is different again. It expresses a scepticism which sounds familiar in the modern world. The author goes by the pseudonym of Qohelet.[19] The book is unusual among the books of the Old Testament in that it seems to convey a very negative message of pessimism. This, however, appears to be a bit of reverse psychology. It is not that we are to accept Qohelet's message on face value. Rather it is a warning from a father to his son (Eccl.12:12) to be careful about the influences in his life.

Tips on Preaching Wisdom Literature

When it comes to preaching wisdom literature, we must take great care. This is not an easy genre to unpack, not least because it is so deep. Despite this, the benefits of dealing with some of the profound questions which are raised by these books are immense.

It is important to bear in mind as you deal with wisdom literature, that it raises more questions than it answers. It is not always possible to get neatly packaged messages which leave the audience feeling satisfied. More often than not these books leave us up in the air. Any attempt to make wisdom sermons more positive and affirming will sound trite. We need to deal with the issues honestly and not try to make light of them. Issues like suffering, death and meaning are dealt with and we need to sense the enormity of these topics, while allowing these books to give us an insight into the issues as they give us their tentative response.

We must also bear in mind that in these wisdom books we are looking in on an open debate. Every word is inspired, but that does not mean that everything that is said by the characters is true. Job's friends, for instance, waxed eloquent about sin and its effects, making a superficial and ultimately incorrect assessment about the reasons for Job's sufferings. The truth needs to be sorted out from the incorrect notions.

We also need to listen to every word of true wisdom which these books highlight. There are many important lessons, especially in Proverbs, that are practical and deal with everyday issues. Ultimately success in life will be determined by the extent to which we live according to wisdom. This wisdom must therefore be identified and communicated.

Gospels

At first glance the Gospels appear to be no more than just narratives. They are, however, unique in their subject matter and contain some complex literary forms as well as definite theological nuances, so they merit a category of their own. The Gospels appear to be biographies of Jesus, yet they are as such incomplete. Neither John nor Mark mention the birth of Christ while the order of events in the life of Christ differ according to which Gospel you read.

Within the Gospels there are also some parables which need to be interpreted separately from the rest of the Gospel material. The parables of Jesus have suffered from a number of erroneous interpretations over the years. Perhaps the best way of interpreting them is to see them as narrative fiction.[20] That is, they are short stories that communicate meaning when studying the perspective of the main characters. This must be done in conjunction with a little allegorising.[21] For example, in the parable of the sower, the sower must be an allegory of Christ in order to make any sense.

If we were to take the parable of the lost son as an example (Luke 15:11-32), we would note that each of the characters have something important to communicate. The son himself teaches us that the best

86

way forward in a situation where rebellion has led to trouble and heartache is to repent. The father in the story teaches us something about the love of God while the older brother tells us something about a begrudging attitude towards God's blessing of others.

Tips on Preaching the Gospels

When preaching the Gospels there are a number of important pointers that we need to be aware of. Firstly, you need to know the general historical context of the Gospels. We read about groups like the Pharisees and the Sadducees. The Gospels mention King Herod, but also Roman governors who exercised great power. We are introduced to a variety of people from tax collectors to terrorists, all of whom contribute to our understanding of the political landscape in Roman-controlled Palestine. There are numerous mentions of local customs as well as hints of the kind of mindset which the people of that day had. All of this information will be necessary for a proper understanding of the Gospel accounts.

Secondly, it is important to discover the motivation of each of the Gospel writers as they penned their words. Even a cursory glance would reveal that each Gospel is distinctly different and intended for a particular audience. Luke's account is methodical and he tells Theophilus, the recipient of the book, that he is trying to put together an orderly account (Luke 1:1-3). John's account is deeply theological and is intended to convince all who read it that Jesus is the Son of God and to bring them to faith (Jn.20:31). Matthew is aiming at Jewish readers and so includes an extensive genealogy of the line of Christ which would impress his readership (Matt.1:1-16). Mark is action-packed and conveyed a dynamic Jesus who is also a suffering servant, and this in turn is linked with discipleship. Once you have discovered the motivation of each writer, their Gospel will begin to make sense.

It is also worthwhile contrasting the Gospels as they have a great deal of material in common. The benefit of harmonising the Gospels is that as we compare the same account in different Gospels we see what makes each distinctive. This will greatly assist our interpretation.

Thirdly, we need to see the theme of the Kingdom of God woven throughout the Gospel accounts. Most Jews in Jesus' day believed they lived on the very brink of time when God would step into human history and usher in a new and better age.[22] This Messianic Age would be a time when God would rule, and there would be peace and righteousness (Isa.2:2-4 ; 11:4-5). This rule of God was often referred to as the Kingdom of God. The study of the end times is known as eschatology, and it was an issue that weighed heavily on people's minds, especially as they were living in times of Roman oppression.

When Jesus began his public ministry he announced that the Kingdom was at hand (Mk.1:14,15) and he proved it by his miracles (Lu.11:20). All eyes were upon him as people wondered if this really was the Messiah, but then he was crucified. After his resurrection there were those who then wondered if he would usher in the Kingdom (Acts 1:6). This did not happen, but he did send the Holy Spirit to help the Christians live out kingdom values in their own lives. The ministry of Christ was therefore not the end of the age, but it was the beginning of the end. The final end will come with his second coming, but in the meantime, in one sense, we do live in the kingdom age.

As far as the Gospels are concerned, we therefore have this tension. The Kingdom has begun and all the ethical teaching in the Gospels demand that we live according to the principles of the Kingdom. But it has not been consummated, so we still live in a fallen world where we struggle with sin and all of its consequences. We need to keep this tension in the back of our minds as we preach the Gospels, and that will enable us to see how the implications of the material can be worked out in our lives.

Epistles

The epistles provide us with some of the most theologically compact texts in the whole of Scripture. They dominate the New Testament and combine for us both private material and material that was intended for public reading.

Although the various writers of the New Testament epistles had their own distinctive style and theology, they followed a general literary pattern which was consistent with the letter writing convention of their day. This contained five main parts:

- Opening greeting
- Thanksgiving (for the memory and wellbeing of the recipients)
- Main content of the letter
- Moral exhortations
- Closing comments

These letters were intended to be read as a whole, and the thought flow or logic of the argument is crucial. Each paragraph builds on the previous one and will lead coherently to the next. They are, however, not detached from the readers as they were also written to address specific people and situations. As we read the epistles we get an insight into what was happening in the early church and what God was saying about it.

Preaching the Epistles

There are a number of pointers that we need to bear in mind when preaching on the epistles. Firstly, we need to take careful note of the verbs and tenses which the writer employs. New Testament Greek is a much more accurate language than contemporary English and is therefore capable of conveying subtle nuances in the text.[23] There are many instances where identifying the correct tense of a verb will have a profound effect on how we read a verse. In Ephesians 5:18, for example, Paul tells the Christians in Ephesus to be 'filled with the Spirit'. In this instance Paul is not referring to a one-off event. The particular tense (present imperative) tells us that this is an activity which must be continuous in our lives.[2]

It is also important that we know the circumstances of the person or people to whom the letter is addressed. As the letters were written to address specific situations, their meaning will be bound up with what those situations are. In a very real sense we as readers are looking over the shoulders of the writer as he pens his message to his intended audience.

Reading an epistle is a bit like reading a postcard that someone else sent to their friend. Only when we know a little of the author's situation, and that of his friend, can we judge what the message is all about. Sometime ago I got a postcard from a friend which went like this:

Dear Stephen,
It makes a real change to be basking in sunshine.
It is also nice to be able to relax a little. Next year
I might not be able to get the chance. Hope all
goes well in Leeds. Send my love to Debbie.

Phil

Superficially anyone could make sense of this postcard. But knowing a little of the background would reveal much more. Once you realise that Phil comes from Scotland but is on his holidays in the Canaries, there is a new appreciation of why he is enjoying the sunshine so much. If you were told that he had just finished his finals at university you would understand why he felt under pressure and you might even guess that he would not have much time to relax in the near future if he got himself a job. Furthermore, if you realised that I was going the following week to Leeds to speak at a conference and that my wife is called Debbie, the last two sentences would make perfect sense.

In much the same way, the circumstances of the writers of the epistles and that of their intended readership sheds a great deal of light on their content.

It is also good to note both the negative and positive instructions in the epistles. Because of the problems which existed in many of the early churches, Paul had to write some pretty stern things to them. He told the Corinthians to 'grow up' and not be childish about the way they use the gifts of the Holy Spirit (1 Cor.14:20). He also warned the Thessalonians not to be lazy and hang about for the Second Coming of Christ (2 Thess.3:10). These negatives contain important principals which contemporary audiences need.

But there are also many positive injunctions in the epistles. In Ephesians 6:10ff Paul tells the Christians in Ephesus to put on the armour of God. Then in Galatians 5:22,23 he urges the Christians there to live out the fruits of the Spirit. Again these are vital lessons for today and should be identified and emphasised in our sermons.

Apocalyptic

One final genre which deserves consideration is that of apocalyptic. This is a form of literature that incorporates vivid and unusual pictures with symbolic meanings. The book of Revelation is a prime example of apocalyptic literature, though not all of the book would contain this genre. The first three chapters, for example, are in the form of epistles written to seven literal churches. These passages need to be treated as epistles. The second part of the book of Daniel is also apocalyptic. Apocalyptic passages cannot be interpreted literally as the ramification of such an interpretation would be absurd.[25]

Apocalyptic literature deals with the end of world history and it comes to the writer in the form of visions and dreams. The subject matter often includes God's answer to the dilemmas of the world, which man has been utterly unable to solve. The symbolism is imaginative, and even bizarre, and it depicts future as well as present events. There is always the battle between good and evil and it is a form of literature designed to encourage people who feel crushed and in need of rescue.

Tips on Preaching Apocalyptic Literature

It is important, when approaching apocalyptic literature, to discover whether the symbolism in the passage would have had any significance to the writer in his culture.[26]

This will demand a great deal of research. The Old Testament itself is a good starting point, for some of the symbols in the book of Revelation can be found in Old Testament times.[27] It is equally important to see if the passage itself gives an explanation of the symbolism. In Revelation 12:9, for example, the passage clearly states that the dragon is the devil, while in Revelation 5:8 we are told that the bowls of incense are the prayers of the saints.

One must also take care when dealing with numerical symbolism in apocalyptic literature. In Revelation we are told about a period of 1260 days or 42 months (Rev.13:5), and about the 144,000 (Rev.14:1). We also read about the great age of 1,000 years, known as the millennium (Rev.20:4), and the army of 200,000,000 men (Rev.9:16). Certainly these numbers mean something, but they are not necessarily meant to be taken literally.

Getting Serious with the Genre

Clearly biblical genre is something to be taken seriously. The many genre of Scripture are complex as well as fascinating. Great care, work and effort, needs to be taken in trying to understand the real message of any given passage. It would be wrong to become scared about approaching Scripture, for after all, the Holy Spirit guides us as we study. But it would be equally wrong to be complacent about studying what is the very Word of God. Spend time thinking about the particular genre you are working with and utilise the many excellent books that are available on the subject of biblical interpretation. These along with good quality commentaries will assist you in discovering the message that has to be preached.

The overarching principle is to discover what the particular passage must have meant to its original readership and then relate that message to a contemporary audience.

As you go through this process there are a number of reminders that you will need to put on a checklist. These are listed, but not in order of importance:

- Remember the importance of discovering what the original language says.
- Allow Scripture to interpret Scripture.
- Don't build a doctrine from an illustration or an ambiguous verse taken out of context.
- Be careful not to spiritualise everything.
- Always think of the intention of the author.
- Recognise that revelation is progressive and that the earliest books of the Bible will not contain a fully-orbed or complete revelation of God or his purposes.
- Differentiate between what is said about Israel and what is said about the church.
- Acknowledge that we are sinful and therefore cannot fully comprehend God's revelation.
- Have the humility to listen to the opinions of mature Christians.

If these guidelines are followed you will be well on the way to understanding the text. Then you can preach it with confidence.

Summary:
- The Bible contains a variety of literary types or genre.
- Narrative is a story, and needs to be preached as a story.
- Biblical Poetry is based primarily on parallelism and makes extensive use of imagery.
- Biblical Prophecy speaks directly into a given situation, as well as containing a predictive element.
- Wisdom Literature delves deeply into the recesses of the human mind, raising issues as well as leaving questions unanswered.
- The Gospels are diaries of the life and teaching of Jesus and they give us ethical guidelines for a fallen world.
- The Epistles are letters written by Christian leaders, which address specific people and situations.
- Apocalyptic Literature uses vivid pictures with symbolic meanings to describe the indescribable.

Points to Ponder:
Try over the next year to preach at least one sermon on each of these genres.

Tools of the Trade

When I was at Bible College, one of my lecturers used to say to the class, 'Next time you want to take your wife out for a meal, don't! Spend the money on books instead.' This may have been a rather extreme statement, and his spouse is unlikely to have agreed with it, but it does emphasise an important fact. Books are crucial in the life of a preacher.

Every tradesman needs his tools, and books are a preacher's tools. Those of us who have English as a mother tongue are uniquely privileged to have such a vast resource available to us. A visit to any Christian bookshop will reveal a wealth of material which we can use in our preaching ministry. It is vital that we learn to use these tools. Using books should be part of our routine in preparing sermons. Without the help of the many books available, our sermons are in danger of being shallow, ill thought-out and opinionated.

Books are expensive so it is not only important to buy books, but also to buy the right ones. Every purchase should be carefully considered. Even though many of the best theological books are expensive, they are a resource that can last a lifetime. Make the investment, but do not allow your books to sit on the shelf gathering dust. Bookcases groaning under the weight of many volumes may look impressive, but they will not contribute to your sermons unless you take the time to use them. My own experience of listening to sermons has confirmed to me that the best preachers are the ones who work hard in their study.

Space would not permit me to give an exhaustive list of all the books which may prove helpful. I would not even have the space to list the books that I have in my own library. What follows, therefore, is a list of the books that I have found to be indispensable and which I believe should form a basic preacher's library. I will endeavour not only to list the books but also to explain why they will be of help.

Bible Versions

It is important firstly to study using several versions. Unless you are well acquainted with the original languages in which the Bible was written, namely Hebrew, Aramaic and Greek, you will not always be able to get the best translation of a verse or phrase. In any case some phrases in the original languages are very hard to translate and that goes some way towards explaining why different English translations vary.

Read whatever passage you are studying in several versions. The comparison between the versions will give you a more accurate idea of what the passage is saying and will often enable you to identify which parts of the text are particularly difficult to translate. I would tend to use the *New American Standard Version*[1] (NASV), the *New International Version*[2] (NIV) and the *Good News Version*[3] (GNV). These three complement each other well. The NASV is a very literal translation, the NIV tends to use dynamic equivalents, while the GNV endeavours to convey the meaning in the kind of language that the average man in the street would use.

As well as having a variety of versions, it is useful to have both an Old Testament[5] and New Testament Interlinear.[6] Interlinear Testaments not only provide a translation of each passage but also provide the Greek text with a literal word-for-word translation underneath. You do not have to know either Hebrew or Greek to benefit from an interlinear, though a little does help. The great benefit is that you will be able to identify the literal translation for each word in the text, and this helps to sharpen the focus of the passage. Working alongside these you will do well to have a Lexicon on the Old Testament[7] and one for the New Testament.[8]

Theological Dictionaries

Once you have got to grips with what the passage is saying by repeated reading, it is time to get down to looking at individual words. Each word is a vehicle which conveys meaning. As Christians we believe that every word is inspired and therefore necessary to convey the full message, so the study of individual words becomes important.

Of course you do not need to study every word which appears in a given passage. You must, however, look closely at all the main words, that is the words upon which the meaning of the text hangs. This is particularly true when looking at sections of the Bible like Paul's Letters, as he makes economical use of words and packs a great deal of theology into every verse. But it is not just Paul's writings that deserve closer inspection. Get into the habit of identifying the key words and keep asking yourself why the author used that particular word.

Once you have identified the key words it is time to use a theological dictionary. A good theological dictionary will tell you the theological significance of words, what their field of meaning is and how that word is used in other passages of Scripture. In short it will be an invaluable asset to your word studies. For the Old Testament I find *The New International Dictionary of Old Testament,* edited by Willem VanGemeren[9] to be the most helpful, and for the New Testament I enjoy Colin Brown's *New International Dictionary of New Testament Theology.*[10] Neither of these multi-volume sets are cheap, but if you obtain them you will probably not need any other books of this kind as they are so detailed.

Concordances

It is also important to use a concordance in your study. A concordance lists words according to their alphabetical order and quotes the line in which that word occurs. It will enable you to identify all the references where a particular word or phrase occurs. You may also be aware of some verse which complements the passage you are speaking on but you cannot remember the reference. Again the concordance enables you to find where that verse can be found.

Most translations have their corresponding concordance so whatever version you use for study, you should obtain the one that relates to it. I use the *NIV Exhaustive Concordance,*[11] edited by Godrick and Kohlenberger, as well as the *New American Standard Exhaustive Concordance of the Bible.*[12] In addition I use the *Exhaustive Concordance of the Bible* by J. Strong[13]. It is based on the Authorised Version of the Bible and enables the reader to link specific Greek and Hebrew words to their corresponding English terms.

Bible Dictionaries and Bible Encyclopaedias

Next you will need to use a Bible dictionary or encyclopaedia. These books are useful for providing information on biblical places, characters, customs and a wide range of biblical topics. You may want more information on King Herod, or perhaps an explanation of the biblical view of evil spirits. It may be that you need some information on Bathsheba for your sermon on David's sin of adultery. All of this will be provided by a Bible dictionary.

My personal favourite is the three volume *Illustrated Bible Dictionary* edited by J.D. Douglas.[14] It is attractively presented, contains many pictures and diagrams, and is very easy to use. It is also thoroughly evangelical. The *International Standard Bible Encyclopaedia* edited by G. Bromiley is also excellent.[15] It comes in four volumes and is virtually exhaustive.

Bible Atlas

One important discipline in Bible study is that of geography. This may seem incidental but with all the place names mentioned in the Bible and the geo-political movements in its storyline, some kind of geographical knowledge is essential.

There are many good Bible atlases to choose from and this being the case it really does not matter which one you opt for. The two that I have used the most are *The Student Bible Atlas*[16] and the *Moody Atlas of Bible Lands.*[17] Both are worth buying and will be useful tools.

Bible History

If biblical geography is important, then biblical history is even more so. The Bible's history takes place over so many years and involves so many events and personalities that the field is a massive one. Because of this there are many books on biblical history and so we need to be very selective.

One of the standard volumes on Old Testament history is *A History of Israel* by John Bright.[18] It is excellent, though I prefer Walter Kaiser's *The History of Israel*.[1] This is more conservative, contemporary and is easy to read, though that fact does not detract from its solidity.

When we come to the New Testament, arguably one of the best books is *New Testament History* by F.F. Bruce.[20] This book begins at the end of the Old Testament period and so brings a continuity to the two Testaments.

It is important not to omit the four hundred years which elapsed between the end of the Old Testament and the beginning of the New Testament. These are crucial years for our understanding of the nation of Israel as portrayed in the Gospel accounts. The best book I have read covering this period is *A History of Israel from Alexander the Great to Bar Kochba*, by H. Jagersma.[2]

Bible Surveys and Bible Introductions

As well as understanding the historical backdrop to a book, it is also important to see where the book lies in the canon of Scripture and to have some background information about the author. To find this you will need to look at Bible surveys and Introductions. In addition to giving you the above information, a good Bible survey or Introduction will note the themes of each book and break it up into its component parts.

Probably the standard Old Testament work over the past twenty years has been *Old Testament Introduction* by R.K. Harrison.[2] It is conservative, detailed and extremely informative. *Old Testament Survey* by Gleason Archer is also a classic.[23] Two more contemporary works which are also excellent are *OT Intro* by LaSour, Hubbard and Bush,[24] and *OT Intro* by Dillard and Longman.[25] Both are well written and are invaluable resources.

As far as the New Testament is concerned, *New Testament Introduction* by Donald Guthrie has done for the New Testament what Harrison's work has done for the Old.[26] A more recent book *New Testament Introduction* by Carson, Moo and Morris is also well worth having.[27]

Biblical and Systematic Theology

As well as being aware of the text itself, it is important to be aware of the theology of the text when preaching. An excellent book on Old Testament theology is *Themes in Old Testament Theology* by William Dryness.[28] It charts the main theological themes of the Old Testament and delivers a good overview. Walter Kaiser's *Toward an Old Testament Theology* is also good and it focusses on the theme of God's promise.[29]

For New Testament study Donald Guthrie's *New Testament Theology* has long been a classic and is highly valuable.[30] Also George Eldon Ladd's *A Theology of the New Testament* is excellent.[31] If brevity is what you are looking for then *New Testament Theology* by Leon Morris is the one to choose.[32] It is not as comprehensive as the other two, but well worth having.

As far as preaching is concerned systematic theology may well not be as important as biblical theology, but it is important to have some good Systematic Theologies at hand. My personal favourite is *Systematic Theology* by Wayne Grudem.[33] It is well written, practical as well as scholarly, and asks useful questions at the end of each chapter. Other volumes worth noting are *Systematic Theology*[34] by Louis Berkhof and *Know the Truth* by Bruce Milne, though the latter is rather brief.[35] It is also worthwhile looking at the three volume *The Evangelical Faith*[36] by Helmut Thielicke and Millard Erickson's *Christian Theology*.[37] The latter, in particular, is becoming very popular.

Background Information

There are also a wide variety of books which give us important background information about the biblical world and the personalities and events within Scripture. The *Peoples of the Old Testament World* is an excellent volume which gives background information on many of the peoples mentioned in the Old Testament.[38] Neal Berling's *Giving Goliath his Due* is also excellent and focusses particularly on the Philistines.[39] Christopher Wright's *God's People in God's Land* is valuable as it provides insights into the Jewish world of family and land ownership.[40]

A useful background to New Testament study is Alfred Edershime's *Sketches of Jewish Social Life*.[41] *Christianity in the Hellenistic World* by Roland Nash looks at the Greek influences in the world of the New Testament and is worth looking at.[42] There is also an excellent book by Ralph Gower on *Manners and Customs of Bible Times*.[43] It is easy to read and very enlightening. An excellent six volume set on the background to the book of Acts edited by Bruce Winter is also available. Though geared specifically to the book of Acts, it provides important background for the whole of the New Testament.[44] All of these books will repay reading and are well worth having in your library.

Biblical Interpretation

Every preacher must learn the art of biblical interpretation, so books which deal with this subject are a must. Bernard Ramm's book *Protestant Biblical Interpretation* is a very good starting place though it is now somewhat dated[45]. *How to Read the Bible as Literature* by Leland Ryken is also very good.[46] More useful than both of these is *How to Read the Bible for all its Worth* by Gordon Fee and Doug Stewart.[47] It is both clear and precise. But the most complete and best book that I have read on the subject is the excellent *Introduction to Biblical Interpretation* by Klein, Bloomberg and Hubbard.[48] It is a must for every budding preacher. There are a number of books which deal with a particular genre. Included in this category are *How to Read the Psalms* by Tremper Longman,[49] *The Wisdom of Proverbs, Job & Ecclesiastes* by Derek Kidner,[50] and *Interpreting the Parables* by Craig Bloomberg.[51] Each of these are good worth obtaining.

Commentaries

No book list would be complete without mentioning commentaries. There are now quite a number of commentary series that cover all or most of the Bible. Most commentary series are a mixed bag with some being better than others. However, in many of the major series there are enough good commentaries to give a warm general recommendation.

When choosing commentaries you must bear in mind that different ones aim to do different things. Some are highly technical and detailed and have comparatively little by way of application. Others are more accessible and apply the text extensively, while others are in the middle category. Of the more technical commentaries I find the *Word Biblical Commentaries* to be useful.[52] This set requires some caution as it is broadly evangelical as opposed to conservatively evangelical, but it is a good series. Some are especially good like the magnificent *Ezra & Nehemiah* by Hugh Williamson.[53] The *New International Commentary on the Old Testament*[54] and the *New International Commentary on the New Testament* are also generally very good.[55]

I also very much like the *New International Greek Text* commentary series, though it is far from complete.[56] The volume on Philippians by P.T. O'Brien is particularly good. This set requires you to have a knowledge of Greek. The *Pillar Commentary* series looks promising, though this is also far from complete.[57]

Of the less technical commentaries the *Tyndale Commentary* series is probably the best all round.[58] But the *Bible Speaks Today* series is also excellent and applies the text well.[59] I have also benefited from the *Daily Study Bible* series.[60] The Old Testament volumes are written by different scholars and are generally quite good. The New Testament volumes are written by the late William Barclay and are excellent for preachers. Some caution is needed with some of Barclay's views but he is always readable and his background information is excellent.

Summary:

- Books are an essential tool for preaching.
- Different versions enable the preacher to understand the text more accurately.
- Theological dictionaries enable the preacher to understand individual words.
- Concordances are useful for cross-referencing.
- Bible dictionaries and encyclopaedias are helpful for background information.
- A Bible atlas will enable the preacher to get the big picture of what is happening in the text, while a Bible history will help him see the significance of an event.
- Bible surveys and introductions give an overall picture of a Bible book, while biblical and systematic theologies help to discover its meaning and relationship to other parts of Scripture.
- Commentaries help the preacher work systematically through a text in detail.

Pause for Thought:

Have a detailed look at your personal library and note the significant gaps. Endeavour to fill those gaps systematically with good books.

9

Putting It All Together

In the previous section we looked at how to study and understand a passage of Scripture. The time has now come to put that understanding into a form that we can convey to others. In short, we need to get the basic structure of the sermon together.

This aspect of the preacher's job is vitally important. A preacher may know his Bible well and understand all the principles of interpretation, but if he does not know how to convey his knowledge to those who listen, the effectiveness of his ministry is greatly diminished. That is why someone who is a good biblical scholar will not necessarily be a good preacher. The job of a preacher is not finished until his message is such that his hearers will understand the content of what he is trying to convey and are challenged to obey.

Many preachers have compared their sermons to house building. In the same way as a house has a foundation, superstructure, front door, windows and a roof, so a sermon should contain all of these features. The foundation of any house is essential. Unless a house is built on a firm foundation it will not last and therefore offers no protection or comfort for those who live in it. The foundation of any sermon is the Word of God. Without the Word being applied, the sermon is of no value to the hearer.

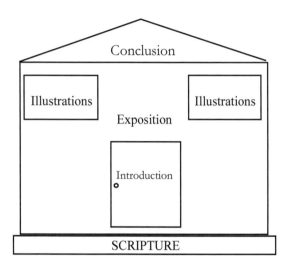

The superstructure of the house is the exposition of the sermon, or the content. This is the major part of the sermon – the central feature to which all other parts point. The front door of the house is the sermon introduction, it gives access to the house. Every house has windows and these are the illustrations that illuminate the points being made in the sermon. A house must also have a roof in order to make it complete. The roof is the conclusion to the sermon. It rounds off everything that has been said so that the package is neat and complete.

It is essential to remember that although introductions, illustrations and conclusions are important, their function is really to highlight the content of the sermon. They in themselves do not constitute the sermon. They are servants and the exposition of the Word is master. Only when the preacher puts them into perspective will his sermon have substance.

Chopping off Chunks

Even before you begin shaping the sermon, you will need to know the passage. Chapters 5 through to 8 have dealt with this issue. By the time that background work has been done, the preacher will have a clear idea of what the passage is saying, and how it relates to the book in which it is found and the Bible as a whole. Now the sermon begins to take shape. The first thing a preacher needs to do is decide how large a passage to preach on. A number of factors come into play at this point. Firstly, you need to consider how much time you will have to deliver the message. It goes without saying that if your allocated time is just thirty minutes, you would never attempt to preach through an entire chapter of a book like Romans.

Secondly, the kind of passage needs to be considered. The Epistles of Paul are very compact and filled with theology and detailed argument. It would be suicidal to take on more than a few verses at a time. The passage would never get full justice. If on the other hand you were to preach through the book of 2 Samuel or Esther, you would need to have a much larger passage to cover. You may even cover a couple of chapters in the one sermon. I have found that the more I preach, the better I become at selecting an appropriate size of passage.

Finding the Theme

The next thing is to find the main theme of the passage. In other words, what is the passage basically about. Having studied the passage in detail, you will probably already know what the theme is. But it is essential to have the theme clearly in your mind, otherwise it will be very difficult to articulate it to and audience. It may well be that the theme which runs through the passage you are studying is the same as the theme which runs through the book as a whole. On the other hand it may be just one of many branches which all make their own distinctive contribution to the broader theme of the book. Whichever of these it is, you will need to have in mind the basic point you want to communicate from this passage.

Once you have this theme clearly in mind, you need to identify how each verse fits into the theme. The passage will be making a number of points which expand on the theme or add to it in some way. Some preachers call the main theme the subject, while they call these individual points the complement.[1] The subject tells you what the passage is basically about while the complement fills out the basic structure with some flesh. This distinction is a useful one.

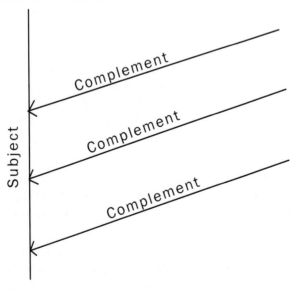

Take the example of the following passage:

'Therefore since we have been justified through faith, we have peace with God through our Lord Jesus Christ, through whom we have gained access by faith into his grace in which we now stand. And we rejoice in the hope of the glory of God.'[2]

You will note that the subject of this passage is 'Justification through' faith. There are a number of complements which add flesh to the basic argument. These are: we have peace with God, it is through the Lord Jesus, we have gained access, this is into his grace, and we rejoice in hope.

I generally find it useful to take a clean sheet of paper and make a note of the subject and then link all the complements with it so that I can visualise in one glance the structure of the whole sermon.

If you have done your homework well, you will have already asked many questions of the text. You will also have used word study books, bible histories and dictionaries to get specific information on the historical backdrop of the passage and the meanings of all the key words. At this point, now that you have identified the structure of the passage, you will find it useful once more to use some commentaries in your study. They will ensure that you are going in the right direction, give accuracy to your exposition, correct any mistakes you have made and perhaps even give you some ways in which you can apply the text.

Once all of that is done you need to think about the layout of your message, that is how you will put it across. Some preachers like to state what their main theme or subject is and then deliver a set number of points in that theme. As they deliver each point they apply it to their audience. This is a good, orderly and neat approach. Others prefer to preach through the passage in the order in which it comes, often verse by verse, applying it as they go along. This layout can also be effective and may well suit particular passages better than the first method. Still others like to deal with the subject by stating what the passage says and then summing up the lessons we can learn from it at the end. Essentially it is a personal choice. I like using all three methods and usually decide which one I use according to the type of passage I am dealing with.

Application

Of course preaching is much more than just communicating information. I have already alluded to the application of the message, and want to do so again because it is so important to the whole job of preaching.

The end result of any sermon should be changed lives. We should never want people to walk away from a sermon saying, 'that was interesting'. Rather we want people to say 'that message really challenged me to do something about my life'. Whether the message is a rebuke, an encouragement, a challenge or a call to a deeper walk with God, there must always be that element that demands action.

Sometimes finding the application is the most difficult thing of all. We may know what God is saying through this passage, but in what way does that apply to the lives of the people in our audience? I would want to make two initial comments at this point. Firstly, I ask myself how does this message apply to my life. If it challenges me in an inconsistent area in my life, then it will probably have the same effect in the lives of people I preach to, as I am probably not much different from them. My experience has been that every time I have ever preached, God has spoken powerfully to me while I was preparing the message. Having found the application that suits my situation, I have used the same application in my sermon and found that members of the audience were going through the same struggle as I was.

Secondly, the point must be made that the most relevant preachers are the ones who know their audience well. I do a great deal of itinerant preaching. There is certainly value in this and I have the freedom when I visit churches to preach boldly, without the audience feeling that I am getting at them. In this sense I am sometimes able to say things that the leaders in those particular churches are unable to say. There is, however, a limitation to itinerant preaching. I just do not know the people I am addressing! They may have been through some church difficulty that I am unaware of. There may be hurting or confused individuals in the audience who are unknown to me. There may be some serious sins being committed by people in the audience that I am ignorant of.

I am not invalidating itinerant preaching, indeed I am deeply committed to it. I also believe that God, who knows everything, often guides my thoughts so that sermons I preach have a piercing relevance to those I am addressing, even though I don't know the situations they are facing. Nevertheless, my lack of knowledge of a particular situation may at times impede my application.

When I preach in my own church, however, the

situation is somewhat different. I know the people who come along. They are not strangers. I have been in their homes and have discussed with them important issues which affect their lives. I will often know what struggles and difficulties they are going through and where they are in their walk with God. So when I preach in my own church, applying the message is not a hit-and-miss exercise. I know what to say, because I know the kind of situations I am addressing.

The lesson is simple! If we want to apply the Word of God to peoples' lives, we need to know the people we are preaching to and the issues that will be relevant to them. It will not do just to have a good knowledge of the Bible and the principles of biblical interpretation. Neither is it sufficient to spend all our time locked in the study doing endless biblical exegesis. We need to be out talking to people and discovering where they are at in their relationship with God, so that our sermons can minister to their needs. In this sense preaching and pastoral work go together and complement each other.

As you are preparing your message, always ask yourself what the real needs of the congregation are. Not that you allow the audience to dictate what you preach, but because you want the message to address their needs. Your application will build the bridge between what the Word of God says, and what it means for those who listen.

Use of Notes
There is one last point that I would make at this stage and it concerns note taking. Perhaps the subject of note taking should be dealt with in conjunction with the issue of the presentation of a sermon. The style of note taking

that you use will to a large extent determine what kind of a presentation you will make to your audience. I want to deal with the issue now, however, because it is part of the process of putting the sermon together.

The issue of notes is important because it is very difficult to remember all that you have studied without at least some prompting. I have a friend who prepares his message and then destroys his notes before he gets to the pulpit so that he can be free from notes to preach more naturally. That is fine if your memory is excellent, or if you are so spontaneous that you can just speak off the cuff. This, though, is very unusual. Most of us need some kind of notes.

It is true, on the other hand, that if a preacher is too tied to his notes, he will be looking down at them constantly, and not at his audience. This is very distracting and a poor way of communicating. The balance must be struck somewhere in the middle.

For myself, I like to use fairly full notes. I type my message in a large font as my eyesight is not brilliant. An average half-hour sermon will require about three to four pages of notes on A4 paper. This might seem a lot to some, but I would rather have too many notes than too few. Experience has taught me not to rely too heavily on my suspect memory. Having said all this, I make sure that I know the message so well that I will not need to look at my notes more than a couple of times per minute, and when I do so it is just a brief glance. I also find that if I have good notes, I have the confidence to be spontaneous when the need arises, and to use them sparingly.

The use of notes is a personal issue and some may wish to use fewer notes than I do. No matter how many notes you use, it is important to remember that it is better to be well prepared than unprepared. Good notes if used wisely will enhance rather than detract from the message.

Only when all this has been done can you begin to think about your introduction, illustrations and the conclusion of your message. That is the subject of the next two chapters.

Summary:
- Preaching a sermon is like building a house with Scripture as its foundation.
- The exposition of the passage is the superstructure of the house.
- The introduction is the door into the sermon.
- The illustrations are the windows, which bring light into the sermon.
- The conclusion is the roof, which finishes off the sermon.
- It is important to apply the passage to the audience.
- Preparing good notes is an important part of the preacher's job.

Pause for Thought:
Analyse some of the sermons you have preached in the past and ask yourself what was missing in them.

10

Introduction and Conclusion

Every house has a front door. It is through this door that a person gains access to the house. Every sermon must also have a point of entry. The front door of a sermon is its introduction. Though brief, an introduction is important because it enables the hearer to enter into the main part of the sermon and understand what the preacher is trying to say.

What does an Introduction Do?

A good introduction should perform four basic tasks. Firstly, it should gain the attention of the listener. Unless the listener is paying attention to what is being said then the sermon is no more than words falling to the floor. The introduction must grab the attention of the audience so that they are in a position to hear what the preacher is saying.

Secondly, the introduction needs to secure interest. This is more than just the initial act of making the person sit up and listen, the preacher will want the audience to keep listening. They must be convinced that the content of the sermon is important, relevant and useful for them. In that sense the introduction is like a fish hook which gets imbedded in the mouth of a fish so that it can be reeled in. Once hooked the fish has little chance of escaping. The introduction must so captivate the listener that he wants to hear all that the preacher has to say on the subject.

Thirdly, the introduction must provide a natural path into the subject matter. The preacher must always remember that the introduction is not an end in itself, but merely a means to an end. It points to the body of the sermon and must prepare the mind of the listener to understand the sermon. This is easier said than done and requires a great deal of precision. If the path into the subject is not straight it will cause confusion. By the end of the introduction, the audience must understand exactly where the preacher is taking them. For this very reason, the introduction is often the last thing that a preacher prepares. This is logical because only when he knows where he is going with the sermon, can he decide the direction in which he wants to point his audience.

Fourthly, the introduction must warm the heart and prepare it to obey. Preachers are not in the business of just conveying a series of detached theological facts. They are appealing to their audience to hear and obey the Word of God. This appeal must start at the beginning of a sermon. In the introduction we want to set an atmosphere that we will want to maintain for the whole sermon. As well as leading our hearers into the subject, we want to encourage them to take action. The introduction should incorporate this motivational content.

Types of Introduction

Bearing in mind the importance of the introduction, we will take some time to think about the different types of introductions than can be used. It is important to be creative and to use a variety of methods to introduce your sermon. There is a sense in which a preacher should never be predictable. If the audience does not know how he will introduce his material, then he is already half-way to securing their interest. The following list demonstrates the variety of introductions that can be used. The list is far from exhaustive, but it may prove helpful:

Illustration/Story

People love stories, both real life and fictional. They can be funny, dramatic or profoundly moving. A story can set the mind racing and once told, it will often be remembered. Stories can therefore be useful tools in introducing the sermon.

Once when preaching on the Cross, I told the story of a young man who died on the battlefield during World War I, fighting to free his country from tyranny. I used this as an inroad to talking about the sacrifice of Christ which frees us from sin. The introduction enabled my audience to understand something of the pain of sacrifice as well as preparing their minds to see the necessity of the death of Christ on the Cross.

Striking Statement

A striking statement can also be powerful as it is startling and it forces people to think about an issue. The statement does not have to be one that you agree with. Sometimes making a statement that is clearly wrong can be useful, provided it is provocative. It can then be unpacked and the sermon itself can demonstrate its flaws.

I remember preaching on the subject of integrity in the Christian life. My first words were 'All Christians are hypocrites', and then I paused for effect. I went on to explain that this statement had been made to me by a young man who was not a Christian, but had several bad experiences in his contact with Christians. The subsequent message challenged the audience to live in such a way as to ensure that this statement could not be made about them.

Proverb

There are many pithy sayings and proverbs which sum up an idea succinctly. These can make excellent introductions as they are often wise sayings which comment on human behaviour. I have frequently used a proverb like 'Give a man fish and feed him for a day, teach him how to fish and feed him for a lifetime', to introduce sermons on the need for a personal devotional life. On one occasion I began a sermon with the proverb, 'You can lead a horse to water but you cannot make it drink', and went on to preach about the need for the Holy Spirit to be involved in our evangelism, as we ourselves cannot make anyone become a Christian.

Question

Questions also make good introductions. They always get people thinking and they demand an immediate response. The more provocative the better. It can be good to ask personal questions and ones which require a lot of soul searching. A carefully thought out question, followed by a pause for effect, can prepare the audience for the answer which your sermon will present.

I can remember preaching on James chapter 1 which deals with the issue of how Christians should respond to suffering. I asked two questions as part of my introduction. The first was – 'Why is life so tough for some Christians, even though they love God?', and the second was – 'How do you respond when your life involves pain and suffering?'. The first of these led the listener to think about why Christians suffer, and the second about our attitude in suffering. Both of these issues are dealt with in the text.

Dramatic Action

If used carefully, dramatic actions can also be effective openers to a sermon. It is important to note that if the action is overly dramatic or in any way inappropriate, it will actually detract from the sermon rather than add to it. It can also get a preacher into trouble. The minister of a nearby church arranged for a friend to dress up like a soldier, brandishing a gun, and to run into the church while he was taking a church service. No doubt he had an important point to make, but he not only scared the wits out of his congregation, he also attracted police attention. Such drama is not to be recommended. If done well, however, dramatic action can be very powerful.

I once preached on the text 'Be still before the Lord and wait patiently for him' (Ps.37:7). I wanted to make the point that in all the busyness and bustle of life we often take little time to be alone with God and calm our hearts before him. For my introduction I merely stood up in the pulpit and waited silently for a few moments, just looking at the audience. When it was obvious to me that they were getting a little uncomfortable with the silence I said 'It is difficult isn't it, just being quiet with no distractions'. The point was made and the sermon then dealt with the importance of being alone with God.

Personal Experience

Our own personal experiences of life can be useful in introducing a sermon. There are many disappointments, happy experiences and salutary lessons which usefully point to how God has worked in our lives. It is important not to focus too much on ourselves. It is also important not to use this kind of introduction to deprecate ourselves in a way that can appear falsely humble, or to overly flatter ourselves. But having sounded a cautious note I highly commend this type of introduction.

I have often begun sermons by talking about some personal struggle that I have had, or some spiritual victory I have experienced. More often than not I have found people in the audience readily identifying with the thoughts I was expressing.

Current Issue

The news also provides us with much material for introductions. The benefit with using news items or current events is that the audience will already be thinking about them and so will immediately feel that what you have to say is relevant and contemporary.

Some time ago I preached on the Second Coming of Jesus Christ. I wanted to emphasise the fact that when he comes, all the evil in this world will be dealt with once and for all. In my introduction I mentioned some of the world's great dictators, including Saddam Hussain who was frequently in the news at that time, and asked how the audience felt about these men who appear to prosper despite their evil deeds. The attention of the audience was arrested and they waited then to hear what the Bible had to say about these men of evil.

Event in History

Someone once said 'History teaches us that history teaches us nothing'. I disagree! There are many lessons in history that have much to teach us if only we are prepared to listen. For this very reason, events in history make good introductions to sermons. Think of some of the great mistakes of history, the heroes and characters of the past, as well as the important developments. All of these provide us with a great deal of material for our sermon introductions.

I preached recently on the text 'If the son shall set you free you will be free indeed' (Jn.8:36). The point of this passage is that true freedom can be found in Christ. In order to force my audience to think about the preciousness of freedom, and the cost that can sometimes be involved in procuring it, I began with the story of William Wallace, the warrior who fought for the freedom of Scotland. The audience happened to be Scottish so the introduction struck a chord.

Where do Introductions Come From?

The biggest problem a preacher faces when it comes to introductions is finding them. Some of us are not naturally creative and so our job is even more difficult. So where do we find good material for sermon introductions? The above list of introductions will give some clue.

Good introductions will come from reading. It is important that preachers do read and read widely. There are many books which I have found helpful, ranging from the Guinness Book of Records to classic novels and Shakespeare. I have been helped by books on philosophy, poetry, history and contemporary life. An active reader will have an active mind and this in turn will help to furnish his sermons with useful introductory material.

It is also useful to read quality newspapers and magazines, watch the news, and listen to good radio programmes. This will enable preachers to keep their finger on the pulse and preach sermons which address contemporary questions. We must always bear in mind that the media will be having a profound effect on the minds of our audience. We can use this to secure their interest when we are preaching, and also to bring God's Word to bear on current events.

Another useful source for introductions is human behaviour itself. Some of the best preachers I have heard are keen observers of human life. They observe how people live, what they do with their time, and then they analyse this. I have heard some wonderful sermon introductions based on subject matter such as how people play sports, how people react when they are sitting by themselves in a restaurant and how people handle criticism. Again the audience will readily identify with this subject material because they see it as being true of themselves.

It will be helpful to think about your own life and experiences and draw from this. Life is so varied and eventful that every person, if they took time to think, could recall important lessons they learned from their own experiences of life. Again these can be used to introduce sermons. Sometimes preachers shy away from using examples from their own experience for they fear that it will be of no interest to the audience. I have found, however, that human stories, however routine, are readily absorbed and do hold people's interest.

The Hidden Danger of Introduction

Having thought through some of the different types of introduction, it is now necessary to spend a little time noting possible dangers that we need to be aware of in this area. I must stress again the importance of the introduction. A good introduction will not only make an audience sit up and take note, it will also make them want to listen to the whole sermon and apply it to their lives.

I think the first and most obvious danger is that of inaccuracy. I have sometimes heard preachers using introductions which involve a good story, simply because it is interesting and not because it leads naturally into the content of their sermon. This is always dangerous because if the introduction leads the listener in one direction and the message in a slightly different direction, confusion can set in. There must be a certain ruthlessness in selecting material for an introduction. Only material which fits within the scope of the objectives I mentioned at the beginning of this chapter should be used. An interesting introduction is not as good as an interesting introduction that leads the listener on a sure path into the content of the sermon.

Another danger is that of over packing the introduction. Again I have heard sermon introductions that have been less than effective because they have been too lengthy and detailed. I remember on one occasion the preacher told such a complex story as his introduction that I was mentally exhausted even before he got to his message. Always keep in mind that the introduction is not an end in itself, but the means to an end. It is the servant of the sermon.

A third danger is the whole issue of time. At a rough estimate, I would say that the introduction should take up approximately 10 per cent of the sermon time. Any flexibility should be towards shortening rather than lengthening this time. Some short introductions can be extremely powerful, but if you take too long, the overall effectiveness of the sermon will be diminished.

And in Conclusion...

Having considered the important issue of the introduction, we now need to spend some time thinking about the conclusion. This part of the sermon is just as important as the introduction, but its function is very different. Whereas the introduction prepares the minds and hearts of the audience to hear the Word of God, the conclusion challenges them to put what they have just heard into practice. If the introduction is the front door of the sermon, then the conclusion is the roof of the sermon, the part of the sermon that brings the whole thing neatly to an end. In the same way that a house without a roof is incomplete, so a sermon with no conclusion is as yet unfinished.

The conclusion of a sermon has three basic functions. Firstly, it should succinctly sum up what has been said so that the audience will remember more easily. Secondly, it should challenge the hearer to respond to the Word of God by obeying it. Thirdly, it should remind the hearer that with God's help, and only with God's help, the content of the message can be lived out.

In much the same way as there are different types of introduction, there are also different types of conclusions. It is important once again to be creative and to think about the must appropriate and powerful way of concluding a sermon. Here are a few examples of conclusions which I have used. Again this is not an exhaustive list, but it may prove helpful:

Revision

A simple going over of the content of the material can be very effective. Obviously this should be brief, but it is both a useful reminder and can be a challenge to obedience. A quick summary will keep the words of the preacher imbedded in the minds of his audience.

Story

It is sometimes helpful to tell a story which illustrates the points made in the sermon and demonstrates the need for obedience. Stories are interesting to listen to, and they are also easy to remember. If a suitable story is used to illustrate the points made in a sermon, people will tend to remember what you have said.

Poem

Poems can also make powerful conclusions. Poetry uses vivid language and often expresses ideas in an emotive way. A good poem will stay in the mind and can sum up an issue succinctly.

Prayer

Prayers can also make good conclusions particularly if they are written rather than off the cuff. The beauty of using a prayer is that it encourages the audience to seek God's help in putting what they have learned into practice in their lives. As well as the preacher saying a concluding prayer, it is also possible to get the whole audience to say one. I have been to several church services where the preacher put a prayer on the overhead projector so the audience could see and participate in a corporate prayer of confession and repentance. In each case this proved to be extremely powerful and moving. It is important to stress that if the members of the audience do not want to be obedient to the Word of God, they should not pray the prayer. This challenges people to make a decision and take action.

You may not want to use a prayer for the whole of your conclusion, but even if you use some other form of conclusion, it is still of great benefit to conclude all of your remarks with prayer.

The Hidden Danger of Conclusion

In much the same way as there are dangers involved in introducing a sermon, there are also dangers in concluding a sermon. It is particularly important that we are aware of these dangers because they can destroy much of the good work that has been done in the sermon.

The first danger is not knowing when to stop. I have often heard good sermons spoiled in this way. The preacher will repeat himself over and over again and I find myself wanting to shout 'Just stop while you can!' Such rambling can make the audience feel frustrated and impatient.

Another danger is taking tangent into another direction. I can remember preaching on a subject and as I was concluding the sermon, another thought which was not related to my subject came to mind, so I mentioned it. This was a mistake. The thought had to be unpacked, and by the time I had finished few people in the audience were thinking about the content of my sermon and much of the impact was lost.

A third danger is that of finishing too abruptly. This will inevitably happen if you have not adequately prepared your conclusion. Any sermon needs to contain an element of appeal. Audiences need to be stimulated into action. Stopping abruptly without bringing some kind of challenge will leave the hearers cold and unsatisfied. On the other hand, if a couple of minutes are spent bringing all your comments to a challenging climax, the effect will be well worth the effort.

Summary:
- Introductions arrest the attention of the audience and bring them into the content of the sermon.
- Illustrations, stories, striking statements, personal experiences and even dramas are all valid forms of introduction.
- Introductions need to be accurate, streamlined and not too long.
- Conclusions sum up the sermon, challenge the hearer and emphasise God's help in matters of Christian living.
- Conclusions should not drag on or go off on a tangent, but neither should they be too abrupt.

Pause for Thought:
Think about some of the most effective introductions and conclusions that you have used. What was it that made them as effective as they were?

11

Opening Windows

I spent most of my early years in Africa. Many of the larger houses in the area where we lived had shutters. It was impractical to have glass windows and the mosquito nets could be easily broken by intruders, so these heavy wooden shutters were an essential safety feature. The problem was that they made the house so dark. Even if there was brilliant sunshine outside, our house was so black inside, one would have no idea what time of day or night it was.

Every morning my father would go around the house and open every shutter. The effect was so dramatic that it was almost magical. In an instant the house was transformed from darkness to brilliant light. Everything could be clearly seen, nothing had to be guessed at. Only someone who lived in a house like that could truly appreciate the enormous value of windows.

If the front door of the house is the sermon introduction, and the roof the conclusion, then the windows of the house are the illustrations. Illustrations are important in a sermon because they bring light, and make things clearly visible. There is nothing more frustrating when preaching a sermon than to see blank faces which clearly demonstrate that the audience really doesn't understand what you are getting at. Well-used illustrations can make the difference between people merely having a vague idea of what you are saying and the message really sinking in.

Illustrations in the Bible

It must be noted that illustrations are thoroughly biblical. The Psalmist uses the illustration of wild grass to demonstrate the mortality of human existence (Ps.103:15), while Jeremiah uses the illustration of a hammer smashing rocks to describe the impact of his message (Jer. 23:29). Jesus himself frequently used illustrations. In Matthew 5:13,14, for example, when talking about the impact he wanted his disciples to make on society, he used the illustration of salt and light. Later in 1 Thess. 2:7 Paul would use the illustration of a mother caring for her children to illustrate his commitment to the Christians in Thessalonica. In each case the biblical writers considered illustrations to be an essential element in the communication process.

What Should an Illustration do?

An important question that needs to be asked concerns the function of illustrations. What is the purpose of an illustration? What do we want it to do for the sermon?

Firstly, an illustration should bring understanding. Some theological concepts are by their very nature difficult to grasp. The doctrine of God, for example, is well beyond the greatest of minds. The mystery of salvation likewise is awesome. The process of sanctification and the act of justification have been the preoccupation of the greatest scholars for centuries. If scholars and great thinkers stagger as they fail to fully grasp such monumental truths, how do preachers communicate them to audiences where many have not developed razor sharp theological minds?

The truth is that we will never be able to understand all of divine truth, let alone communicate it. But we will be greatly assisted in our task by using illustrations that convey these theological concepts in language that people will readily comprehend. Illustrations will take ideas that are complex and transfer them into word pictures that can be assimilated and appreciated.

Secondly, illustrations can bring clarification. It is important that others understand what we are saying. This is particularly so when dealing with the word of God. We need precision so that no ambiguity will exist. Again illustrations can do this. A precise idea can be pinpointed in such a way that the audience knows exactly what the preacher is getting at.

Thirdly, illustrations retain interest. Even the most dynamic and absorbing of speakers will not find it easy to retain an audience's attention span for even half an hour. Those of us who are less absorbing will find the job an even harder struggle. The sermon is a vehicle which conveys God's message, but if illustrations are added, the journey is all the smoother. Good illustrations peppered throughout a sermon will not only ensure people understand, they will also help to keep their attention. Only when people are listening to the sermon can they benefit from it, so this function of an illustration should not be ignored.

Finally, illustrations should enthuse an audience. The preacher should make his audience excited about the subject matter. He should demonstrate that obeying God's Word and living the Christian life is the best thing to do. Illustrations can bring a sermon to life and move the audience into action.

What Illustrations Shouldn't Do!

Although illustrations are a useful tool, we need to remember that they are only that. Illustrations are not the message, they merely help the message by making it understandable. There are some dangers that we need to be aware of as we develop our illustrations.

Illustrations that take over

Firstly, we need to ensure that our illustrations do not take over the whole message. I have all too frequently made the mistake of using too many illustrations in my preaching, and this has usually happened when I have not done enough work in studying the text. It is a big temptation to have a lot of illustrations, firstly because they take up time and compensate for a lack of preparation, and secondly because they hold people's attention. If they take over, however, we will end up giving our audience lots of nice stories but very little spiritual food.

I have come to the conclusion that there should be only one illustration for each point in my sermons and a sermon should never have more than seven or eight illustrations. I also feel that if you need lots of stories to make your sermon worth listening to, you should not be a preacher. Too many illustrations provide a poor diet for the church and a poor use of preaching time.

Illustrations that draw the audience away

Secondly, we need to watch out for illustrations that take the audience's mind away from the points you are making in the sermon. There are obvious reasons why this happens. A preacher can use an illustration that does not really fit in with the point being made. It is inaccurate and therefore deflects the listeners from the point, or simply confuses them. Make sure you find illustrations that fit the points you are making rather than finding points that fit the illustrations you want to use.

It is also possible that the illustration you choose is so memorable that it is all that the listener can remember. I once preached on sin and was making the point that the Bible describes us as prisoners to sin (Gal.3:22). I told a gripping story to illustrate this point and hoped that the message would hit home with great force. Later I discovered that most of the people who were listening to the message could remember the story I told, but had no idea what the point of my message was. Clearly this was a mistake.

Illustrations that are inappropriate

Thirdly, we need to be careful not to use illustrations that are inappropriate to our audience. This presupposes that you know your audience and can identify the kind of things that would appeal to them. If the point of an illustration is to communicate, then you need to use illustrations that your audience can readily identify with.

I once heard a preacher use an illustration about the life of a leading dance music DJ. His audience was composed mostly of elderly people who didn't know what a DJ was, so they simply did not understand the point he was making, even though a younger audience would have. The problem was not that it was a bad illustration, but that it was the wrong one for that particular audience. On another occasion a preacher used an illustration taken from the Second World War, but as few of the members of his audience were born then, it was lost on them. Always know your audience and choose illustrations that they will be able to identify with.

Where Do Illustrations Come From?

Again the question needs to be asked, where can good illustrations be found? The answer is, almost everywhere! Stories that you have read, lines from poems, current events, proverbs, all of these can be used to illustrate the points you are making. The Bible itself is also full of illustrative material. I have often found myself drawing from the many stories in the Old Testament in my illustrations.

One friend of mine, who is a marvellous preacher, always looks at billboards and advertising hoardings in the hope of finding good illustrations. Indeed, when he and his wife are out in the car, she does the driving while he writes down any useful ideas which he sees on billboards in a notebook which he always carries with him. He also notes down ideas from TV adverts and the programmes themselves. It does not take him all that long to fill a notebook, and he now has dozens of them. These provide him with a goldmine of illustrations for his sermons.

I have another friend who, whenever she hears an interesting story or some true life experience, says, 'there is a sermon illustration in that'. She is absolutely right. More often than not these accounts can easily be brought into a sermon to illustrate something. On one occasion another friend of mine had lost his baggage on a trip to an Eastern European country. Though the people he was staying with during his trip were poor, they all donated articles of clothing so that he could have a change of clothes. When I related this story to my friend she immediately remarked, 'there is a sermon illustration in that'. Within days I found myself preaching on Christian love and I used that illustration as part of my talk.

One of the most important habits to get into is that of collecting sermon illustrations. You may, like my friend, want to keep a notebook with you at all times, or perhaps have a file at home where you put illustrations that you come across. Once your collection begins to grow you may want to categorise your illustrations under different headings to facilitate easy access. However you collect illustrations, make sure that you do. It will take a certain amount of discipline, for without consciously building up a bank of illustrations, you will never have a ready source. Work hard at it. You may even want to buy one of the many books of illustrations that are now available. Use every available source so that your sermons are enriched.

The important thing to remember is creativity. Never be afraid to use any illustration, provided it does not take over, or draw the audience away and is not appropriate to your audience. Use your imagination. Pepper your sermons with good illustrations and they will develop life, vitality and clarity.

There are a few final remarks that need to be made about illustrations. Firstly, any illustration that needs extensive explanations should not be used. This may seem an obvious thing to say, but I have often witnessed preachers using an illustration and then saying, 'by that I mean...'If you need to explain an illustration, then it will hardly assist you in making the passage of Scripture clear, so save yourself the hassle and don't use it.

Secondly, be careful about using people that the audience know personally in your illustrations. I know of one situation where a pastor was involved in a counselling situation and used the problem that he was dealing with as his illustration. He attempted to be subtle and used a pseudonym rather than the person's real name and spoke in a detached way so that his audience would think this issue happened a long time ago in another church. The people he was preaching to were not as stupid as he was, however, and they all guessed who he was talking about. The situation was disastrous.

Thirdly, if you use quotations in your illustrations, ensure that you name the person you are quoting from. Also try not to quote from people that the members of your audience will never have heard of. Naming the person is important because you should never take the credit for another person's wise words. Quote from people the audience knows are important because then the quotation will have greater impact and you will not sound like an intellectual snob.

Fourthly, get your facts right when using illustrations. I once heard a preacher saying that when a person has a disturbing dream, like falling off a tall building and hitting the ground, the dream itself can kill them. He boldly declared that this had been proved from science. Such nonsense is not only laughable, it damages the credibility of the preacher. Be careful not to make too many 'scientific claims' if you do not know your science very well.

Finally, keep your illustrations short and punchy. Jesus told the Parable of the Lost Coin and applied it in just 73 words. We can learn a great deal from the master storyteller!

Summary:

- Illustrations should bring understanding, clarity and interest to a theological point.
- Illustrations should not take over, draw the audience away from the theme, or be inappropriate.
- Illustrations can come from books, the media, current events and everyday life.
- It is important to think creatively about illustrations.

Pause for Thought:

Try to develop a system for gathering and categorising illustrations so that you will have a bank of them to use in your sermons.

12

The Presentation

Even when the passage has been well studied, a sermon constructed complete with appropriate introduction, illustrations and a conclusion, there still remains one more thing that needs to be considered. I am referring to the presentation of the sermon. People are very inclined to be influenced by their first impressions. How a preacher presents himself to his audience is therefore an important part of his work. If his overall presentation is not good, his audience will make snap judgments about him, and consequently his message. Everything from his deportment to the tone of his voice could potentially be a barrier to his audience hearing and appreciating what he has to say.

In the world of retail, a great deal of time is spent in the presentation of a commodity. Cars in the showroom are polished until they gleam, a piece of jewellery in a shop window will be well positioned beneath lights which will ensure that the gems sparkle, and clothes are presented and mounted on shapely mannequins. The reason for all of this is not because manufacturers and retailers have little confidence in their products. On the contrary, they know that what they are selling is good, and because it is good, they want to package it in such a way as to make the customer take note.

Preaching also involves presentation. The 'product' that we have to offer is the Word of God. It is invaluable and essential to the lives of our audience. But if it is not packaged well, the audience will not fully appreciate it. This is where presentation becomes important. Present the Word of God well and people will readily see and appreciate it. Ignore presentation, and the effect will be lessened.

I have been to services where members of the audience have been distracted by the preacher's bad haircut and clothes that look like they came from a hard-done-by charity shop. I have myself struggled to appreciate a sermon because of the lack of attention the preacher has given to the way he speaks, or simply because he has some annoying mannerism. I am not for one minute justifying this weakness which is all too real in most churches. But the reality is that people easily lose concentration or are put off by relatively small distractions. Time spent in thinking about presentation, therefore, is time well spent. If sharpening up on my presentation will mean that my audience will be able to concentrate on the message, then it is a small sacrifice to make.

Non-Verbal Communication

It is important to realise that non-verbal communication is actually very powerful. If you preach about joy but your face shows no sign of it, the audience will struggle to take your message seriously. When preaching a message which appeals to the audience to get excited about something, but your mannerisms in themselves convey no excitement, then the effect of the message will be diluted. Actions do speak much louder than words. The way that we say things, therefore, is almost as important as what we say.

Of course non-verbal language does not just have a negative impact on the audience, its impact can also be positive. Our body language and our general persona can dramatically enhance our communication. Good presentation can do as much good as bad presentation can do harm.

Dressed to Preach

When we think about presentation, there are a number of issues that need to be taken into consideration. Firstly, there is the way we dress. Preachers can sometimes make such an issue of dress codes that they become overly pristine. Churches too can put such a lot of stress on dress codes, that they become intimidating and unwelcoming places. Some churches positively alienate outsiders because of the 'fashion parade' that occurs each Sunday. This is wrong and should be guarded against. However, the issue of dress is still worth considering.

The best principle to apply to the way a preacher dresses is to say that he should blend in with the crowd. He should not wear anything that would get him noticed or encourage the audience to talk about his clothes rather than his message. This works both ways. In a church where people dress up and where ties and jackets are the norm, it would be out of place for the preacher to wear jeans and a T-shirt. On the other hand, in a church where most people come casually dressed, the preacher should not wear a three piece suit and tie.

It is not that clothes in themselves are an issue. There is no set way to dress for church and if we invent dress codes for our churches we will become legalistic. The Bible says nothing about how we dress during corporate worship. The point is, however, that the preacher's message should be what is noticed, not his appearance. If he looks appreciably different from his audience, it might end up being the other way around.

Body Movements

The next thing to think about is body movements. We are human beings, not inanimate objects, and movement is very much part of every day life. It would be very unnatural if we all just stood motionless for any length of time, and if a preacher were to deliver his sermon while standing absolutely motionless, it would certainly look strange.

I can remember as a boy being taken to a nearby church by my parents, to hear a visiting preacher. In all honesty, I cannot remember a single thing that was said during the course of the sermon. What I do remember is that the preacher stood upright with his hands clasped behind his back the whole time. There was not a single movement, even his lips barely moved. If it were not for the fact that some sounds were coming from his direction one might well have assumed he was dead. The fact that I remember nothing of what was said, but vividly remember the lifeless way in which he said it, speaks volumes about that kind of preaching.

What we need to bear in mind is that there are two kinds of movements. The first is 'involuntary movement', and the second is 'deliberate movement'. Both need to be taken into consideration. Involuntary movements are part of what we are. We communicate not only by what we say but also by our actions. Some people are a great deal more expressive than others and this can be seen in the movement of their hands, their facial expressions as well as general body movements when they are speaking. Some cultures are more expressive than others, and people within those cultures tend to talk in a much more animated way than those from more reserved cultures. There is nothing wrong in this, it is just the way we are.

The difficulty comes if our involuntary movements are so pronounced that they are a distraction to the audience being addressed. Standing in front of people and preaching is very stressful. It is difficult to relax when you are in the pulpit, and this is where the problem lies. Nervousness has the side effect of exacerbating involuntary movement. A person may not have any noticeable body movements in normal conversation, but if he stands in front of an audience, every movement is accentuated. We need to be aware of this.

I wear glasses. On one occasion a kind friend told me that when I preach, I readjust the position of my glasses every ninety seconds or so. That means that during the course of a half-hour sermon, I would do this about twenty times. I had no idea that I did this, but it must have been a distraction to those who were listening. I know one preacher who not only twitches his head violently and with great regularity, he also scratches his head and even his armpits while in the pulpit. I even know of a preacher who used to remove a pencil from the inside pocket of his jacket while preaching, and use it to clean out his ears.

Not all involuntary movements are as obvious and extreme as these examples. It is also impossible to completely stop every squint, twitch and jerky movement. We must, however, be aware of them and endeavour to keep them to a minimum. One thing that I found very hard, but helpful, was to preach in front of a mirror just to see what I looked like while in action. I don't recommend that you do this regularly because you will end up not wanting to preach at all. But it is an effective way of making you aware of involuntary movement.

The second type of movement is deliberate movement. That is movements which we deliberately, and consciously make, in order to aid our verbal communication. Body language is extremely important. It can be a great asset to our preaching. Whether it is to raise your hands, clench your fists, point or shake a finger, clap, stamp your feet, or lean right over the podium, each of these if done well can add considerable power to what you are saying.

There is no set way of using deliberate movements, and no exhaustive list. Our personalities should dictate how we use this form of non-verbal communication. There are, however, a few suggestions I would wish to make. Firstly, make sure you vary your deliberate movements. Resist the temptation to use just one type of movement, otherwise you will become stereotyped and this body language will loose its power. Secondly, never use deliberate movement in any half-hearted way, make it deliberate, or the audience will think you lack confidence and conviction. Thirdly, get your timing right. Good timing will make the difference between a powerful non-verbal communication and a very ordinary one.

Eye Contact
Another form of body language is eye contact. This is extremely important when preaching. Having sat and listened to many preachers over the years I can

confidently state that a preacher who never looks at his audience is one who is hard to listen to.

Eye contact is important for several reasons. Firstly, it involves the audience and therefore keeps their concentration. As you look at individuals, you engage with them and they listen more carefully. Secondly, it makes those people with whom you make eye contact feel that you are speaking to them. Eye contact can ensure that you are dealing with people on a personal level, even though your audience may be very large. Thirdly, when you make good eye contact you are projecting yourself more powerfully and thus a point can be made much more forcefully.

Of course if you use a great deal of eye contact, you will not be able to look at your notes as much. This is not easy, particularly if you are inexperienced or lack confidence. You will need to compensate for this by getting to know your material well before you preach. You also need to avoid making too much eye contact with any one person. I try to make eye contact with everyone in the audience at least once. This might be impossible if the audience is very large, but I have found that during a half-hour sermon I can certainly make eye contact with over one hundred people.

The Voice

The voice itself is worthy of attention. Speech is much more complex than just words. Our voice can convey both feelings and ideas. Whether we are angry, excited, despondent or simply tired, all of these are reflected in our voice.

It is important, therefore, to think about how we use our voices as we preach. There is nothing more boring than a preacher droning on in a lifeless voice. Neither is there anything less awe-inspiring than a sermon in monotone, it is guaranteed to put the audience to sleep. It is also impossible to convey urgency and excitement unless the voice is used to good effect.

There are a number of very simple methods of using the voice which will transform a sermon. Firstly, vary the tone. By allowing the voice to go up and down the scale, it is possible to inject life and urgency to anything that is said. In one sense varying the tone is a little like playing music. If a flute player were to play only one note it would not be long before the sound would become unbearable. Varying the notes, however, can produce beautiful music. In much the same way, varying the tone of the voice produces a verbal tune that is both pleasant to listen to and meaningful.

Secondly, it is important to pause at particular points. My wife once told me that silence can be as meaningful as speech. I now know what she means. I have a friend who is a compulsive talker. He literally never stops from the moment we meet until the moment we part. I confess I get annoyed with him sometimes. It is not just because I can never get a word in edgeways. When a person talks incessantly, it is hard to listen and to concentrate. The volume of vocabulary does not mean that he has communicated with me. Quite the reverse. Listening to that constant flow of sounds is just exhausting and I struggle to take it all in.

Sometimes my preaching is a little like that. I talk very quickly (due to nervousness) and so at times my sermons are just a flood of words, so overpowering that they drown rather than refresh. Taking the time just to pause, on the other hand, brings real power to a sermon.

A pause will give an audience the opportunity to think and reflect. It will give emphasis to a particular phrase that you want to highlight. A pause is truly versatile because it can be placed before a particular phrase, after it or both. In each case it will give the desired effect.

Many preachers are afraid of silence. They rationalise in their own minds that they need to keep up the flow of words in order to maintain the attention of their audience. This is not the case. Sometimes when preachers decide to use a pause, they are so reticent that it ends up being very short and may as well not have been there in the first place. A pause will not seem as long to the audience as it will to the preacher. A confidently used pause will make the audience sit up and take note.

Another way of using the voice is to raise it at appropriate moments. I am not advocating shouting! To be honest I do not like preachers who shout their way through a message. Volume must not be equated with power, the two are certainly not the same thing. Indeed, some of the most powerful preachers I know are really very quiet when they preach. Nevertheless, raising the voice does create the idea that what is being said is particularly important. It is therefore appropriate at relevant parts of the message to put great stress on what is being said by raising the volume to an energetic level.

The reverse is also true. A very effective device is to lower the voice, even to the point where the audience has to listen carefully just to hear what is being said. If this is done while leaning into the microphone it can create the kind of atmosphere in which it is possible to hear a pin drop. This is what I call powerful whispering. If coupled with a raised voice at other parts of the message, the effect will be considerable.

Summary:

- However good the content of a sermon might be, its effect will be lessened if the presentation is not good.
- Non-verbal communication makes the initial impact.
- Appropriate body movements and good eye contact will emphasize the message and keep the audience's attention.
- Altering the tone of the voice and using the voice for emphasis makes for easy listening.

Pause for Thought:

The best way of perfecting your presentation is to video yourself preaching, either to a live audience or in private, and then analyse yourself. It is a painful thing to do but will produce dividends.

13

Preach the Word

I have now been actively involved in church life for over sixteen years. It has been my privilege, and pleasure, not only to be a church member, but also a member of a number of different churches. In the course of my itinerant ministry I have preached in many different churches, both in the United Kingdom and abroad. At the moment, I have the privilege of being an elder in a small, and fairly new church, just a few miles away from my home in Motherwell. As a result of these experiences I am not unfamiliar with church life. This first-hand experience of churches has convinced me of one thing. We need a new generation of good preachers!

Preaching is not a fashionable thing these days. The truth is that there are so many jokes about preachers circulating in many of our churches, I sometimes get the impression that preachers are looked upon with a little disdain. The sermon too seems to be losing its appeal. In many churches it is squeezed into an ever smaller space within the church service, and the preacher dare not go over his allocated time. It is forgivable if we sing one hymn too many or if the children's item runs a minute or two over. No one will mind if the drama presentation is a little longer than expected. People will tolerate lengthy and rambling announcements. But if the preacher takes too long, there is big trouble!

Perhaps I am overstating things a little, but not by much. I have frequently looked down at my audiences when preaching, and noticed how often people check their watches. On those rare occasions when I have gone over my time, I have monitored the increasing restlessness with every minute that goes by. On one occasion I even had a person walk out during my sermon because I went three minutes over the allocated time. One wonders what urgent business that person had, that forced him to exit so quickly. The reality is that in some churches the weekly sermon has been relegated to such a lowly position, it has become barely more important than the coffee break.

This attitude towards both the sermon and the preacher is one which must be challenged at all costs. The exposition of the Word of God is so fundamental to the life of a church, that it is simply impossible for a church to remain spiritually healthy without preaching.

The problem is that if both preacher and sermon are undervalued, there will eventually be a shortage of both. Preaching is hard work! There is the toil of preparation, many lonely hours spent digging into Scripture to discover what God is saying. This is followed by more hours spent discovering the best way of applying the message to a contemporary audience. Then there is the stress of getting into the pulpit to present the sermon to the church congregation. Exciting? Certainly! A joy? Yes! But far from easy. If, at times, the congregation responds with a mixture of indifference and unresponsiveness, then discouragement can set in. It is this discouragement that we need to guard against.

As we enter the pulpit, we become God's heralds, declaring the wonders of his will to all who would listen.

This is a great privilege, and a noble task. When writing to the Galatians Paul declared that God had 'revealed his Son to me, that I might preach Him among the gentiles'.[1] Being a preacher is a calling. It is a calling to stand firm against all pressure and to declare boldly what God is saying to his people and to the world. It is a calling that requires courage, integrity and a sense of purpose. God's messenger must live out his message as well as preach it, and he must preach it with conviction, knowing that it is the truth. His mandate does not come from a church or denomination, but from God himself. Such is the awesome responsibility that being a preacher entails.

This is a task which will sort out the men from the boys. The true men of God will rise to the task, while those who are boys will shrink from it. This is indeed a test of true Christian character. To preach the Word, in season and out of season, is to stand for what is right. When we preach truth in a society that is utterly corrupt, and in a church that will all too easily accommodate the pervasive nature of that society, we declare that God has another way for men to live. We thus engage in a great cultural war, the culture of this world against the counter-culture of Christianity. In this battle, preaching will always have a role, it is one of the church's most powerful weapons. Through preaching we can confront the church's complicity with the world, and the world's sinfulness. Preaching will be a double-edged sword, and the preacher a warrior for truth. The two will do battle, and by the grace of God will prevail. The Word of God, boldly declared, will have its impact, and bring glory to God.

Today the church urgently needs a new generation of preachers! Who will rise to the task?

Summary:

- Preaching is increasingly under siege in the modern church.
- There is presently a great need for gifted preachers who will fearlessly declare God's word.

Pause for Thought:

Ask God to anoint your ministry so that you will be a key voice in today's church, declaring the word of God.

• Appendix 1 •

Practising your Introductions

Imaging you are preaching on the following passages. Try and think of the best way of introducing the subject.

John 3:1-16   Jesus' conversation with
                       Nicodemus

Genesis 39:1-20   The temptation of Joseph

Isaiah 40:28-31   Gaining strength from God

Ephesians 6:10-20   The armour of God

Daniel 1:1-21   Daniel in captivity

Exodus 20:1-16   The Ten Commandments

Hosea 11:1-11   The love of God

Hebrews 11:1-12   Faith

Practising your Illustrations

Imagine you are dealing with the following verses in a sermon. Think of the best way of illustrating them.

Philippians 2:3   'Do nothing out of selfish ambition...'

Ephesians 4:2   'Be completely humble...'

Matthew 7:16   'By their fruits you will recognise them.'

Psalm 27:1   'The Lord is my Light...'

Philippians 2:6   'Who, being in very nature God, did not consider equality with God something to be grasped.'

Proverbs 29:1   'A man who remains stiff-necked after many rebukes will suddenly be destroyed without remedy.'

Genesis 40:23   'The chief cupbearer, however, forgot Joseph.'

Revelation 2:2   'I know your deeds, your hard work, and your perseverance.'

Preaching Assessment Sheet

The Content and Organisation of a Sermon

Please tick each point if it applies:

Introduction:
Did the introduction arrest attention? ____
Was the introduction relevant to the sermon? ____
Was the introduction of reasonable length? ____

Subject:
Was the subject of the sermon made clear? ____
Was the subject relevant to the audience? ____

Outline:
Was there a logical sequence of thought? ____
Were the main points distinct? ____

Development:
Was there good interpretation of Scripture? ____
Was there a smooth transition between points? ____

Illustrations:
Were points illustrated appropriately? ____
Were illustrations concise and to the point? ____

Application:

Was there appropriate application? ____

Was there sufficient application? ____

Conclusion:

Was the sermon summarised well? ____

Was the conclusion a suitable length? ____

Did the conclusion call for a clear response? ____

Voice:

Was the voice sufficiently loud? ____

Was there a good variation in tone? ____

Enthusiasm:

Was the presentation enthusiastic? ____

Was there good eye contact? ____

Did the speaker communicate naturally? ____

Closing Comments: _____

_____

_____

_____

_____

Notes

Chapter 1

1. Peter Adam, *Speaking God's Words*, (Leicester: IVP, 1997), p.38.
2. David Norrington, *To Preach or Not to Preach*, (Paternoster, 1996), p.5.
3. Ibid., p.4.
4. Gordon Fee, *1&2 Timothy*, NIBC, (1990), p.283.
5. Justin Martyr, *First Apology*, The Ante-Nicene Fathers, Vol.1, (Eerdmans, 1993), p.186.
6. Eusebius, *The History of the Church*, (Dorset, 1965), p.148.
7. John Stott, *I Believe in Preaching*, (Hodder, 1982), p.21.
8. Roland Bainton, *Here I Stand*, (Lion, 1988), p.349.
9. John Calvin, *Institutes of the Christian Religion*, (Battles trans., Westminster), p.1023.
10. Ibid., p.1023.
11. Ibid., p.348.
12. J.I.Packer, *Among God's Giants*, (Kingsway, 1991), p.368.
13. Richard Baxter, *The Reformed Pastor*, (Banner of Truth, 1997), p.147-148.
14. John Pollock, *George Whitfield*, (Lion, 1972), p.248.
15. Tony Sargent, *The Sacred Anointing*,(Hodder & Stoughton, 1994), p.19.
16. Ibid., p.43.

Chapter 2

1. WWW.barb.co.uk/tv facts/story.cfm
2. Social Trends 28, p.218.
3. Ibid., p.218.
4. Fact File 2000.
5. Ibid., p.217.
6. Ibid., p.217.

Chapter 4
1. Haddon Robinson, *Expository Preaching*, (Leicester: IVP, 1999),p.20.

Chapter 5
1. James 1:1-8, NIV.

Chapter 6
1. William Klein, Craig Bloomberg & Robert Hubbard, *Introduction to Biblical Interpretation*, (Word, 1993), p.187.
2. Don Carson, *Exegetical Fallacies*, (Baker, 1989), p.35.
3. P.E. Hughes, *The Book of Revelation*, (IVP, 1990), p.44.
4. PT O'Brien, *Commentary on Philippians*,(NIGTC, Eerdmans, 1991), p.354.
5. Ibid., p.200.
6. Ibid, p.174.

Chapter 7
1. Leland Ryken, *How to Read the Bible as Literature*, (Academic Books, 1984), p.33.
2. *The Concise Oxford English Dictionary.*
3. Ibid., p.87.
4. Andrew Hill & John Walton, *A Survey of the Old Testament*, (Zondervan, 1991), p.248.
5. William Klein, Craig Bloomberg & Robert Hubbard, *Introduction to Biblical Interpretation*, (Word, 1993), p.225.
6. Henry Virkler, *Hermeneutics*, (Baker, 1981), p.106.
7. Tremper Longman III, *How to Read the Psalms*, (Leicester: IVP, 1988.), p99-105 Longman provides us with a list of different parallelisms, all of which I have included with the exception of synthetic parallelism for which there is little justification.
8. Ibid., p.241.
9. Ibid. p.24-34. Longman provides a definition of the different types of psalms.

10. Denis Lane, *Preach the Word*, (Evangelical Press, 1986), p.60.

11. Willem VanGemeren, *Interpreting the Prophetic Word*, (Zondervan, 1990), p74.

12. Ibid., p.292-299. Kline, Bloomberg and Hubbard provide us with a list of different types of prophetic revelation, some of which I have included.

13. Grant Osborne, *The Hermeneutical Spiral*, (Leicester: IVP, 1991)

14. Bernard Ramm, *Protestant Biblical Interpretation*, (Baker, 1997), p.246.

15. Derek Kidner, *The Wisdom of Proverbs, Job and Ecclesiastes*, (Leicester: IVP, 1985), p.11.

16. Ibid., p.12.

17. Raymond Dillard & Tremper Longman III, *An Introduction to the Old Testament*, (Leicester: Apollos, p.1985), p.201.

18. Ibid., p.235.

19. Ibid., p.248.

20. Ibid., p.338.

21. Craig Blomberg, *Interpreting the Parables*, (Leicester: Apollos, 1990), p.68.

22. Gordon Fee & Douglas Stuart, *How to Read the bible for all its Worth*, (Milton Keynes: Scripture Union, 1983), p.118.

23. Ibid., p.65.

24. Andrew Lincoln, WBC, *Ephesians*, p.344.

25. Ibid., p.268.

26. Ibid., p.269.

27. Compare Revelation 10:9-11 with Ezekiel 2:9-3:9.

Chapter 8

1. *American Standard Version*, Holman Bible Publishers.

2. *New International Version*.

3. *Good News Bible*, The Bible Societies/Harper Collins.

4. Dynamic equivalents is a term used to describe the translation of a text using words that convey the particular meaning of the passage rather than a literal word for word translation. At times a word for word translation will actually obscure the meaning of the text because of the different ways in which different languages use vocabulary.

5. *The NIV Interlinear Hebrew-English Old Testament*, ed.J.R. Kohlenberger III, (Regency, 1987).

6. *The NIV Greek-English New Testament*, Alfred Marshall, (Zondervan, 1976).

7. *Concise Hebrew and Aramaic Lexicon of the Old Testament*, (W.L. Holladay, Leiden, 1971).

8. *The Analytical Greek Lexicon Revised*, Harold Moulton, (Regency, 1978).

9. *New International Dictionary of Old Testament Theology and Exegesis*, Ed. Willem VanGemeren, (Paternoster Press, 1997).

10. *The New International Dictionary of New Testament Theology*, Ed. Colin Brown, (Paternoster Press, 1986).

11. *The NIV Exhaustive Concordance*, Edward Goodrick & John Kohlenberger III.

12. *New American Standard Exhaustive Concordance of the Bible*, (Nashville, T.N. Holman, 1981).

13. *Exhaustive Concordance of the Bible*, James Strong, (Hodder & Stoughton, 1936).

14. *Illustrated Bible Dictionary*, Ed.J.D. Douglas, (IVP, 1980).

15. *International Standard Bible Encyclopaedia*, Ed.G. Bromley, (Eerdmans, 1979).

16. *The Student Bible Atlas*, (Candle Books, 1995).

17. *The Moody Atlas of Bible Lands*,B Beitzel, (Moody Press, 1985).

18. *A History of Israel*, J.Bright, (Westminister, 1981).

19. *A History of Israel*, Walter Kaiser, Broadman & Holdman, 1998.

20. *New Testament History*, F.F. Bruce, (Doubleday, 1972).

21. *A History of Israel from Alexander the Great to Bar Kochba*, H. Jagersma, (SCM, 1985).

22. *Introduction to the Old Testament*, R.K. Harrison, (IVP 1969).

23. *A Survey of the Old Testament Introduction*, Gleason Archer, (Moody, 1985).

24. *Old Testament Survey*, LaSor, Hubbard & Bush, (Eerdmans, 1982).

25. *An Introduction to the Old Testament*, R. Dillard, T.Longman, (Leicester: Apollos, 1995).

26. *New Testament Introduction*, Donald Guthrie, (Leicester: IVP, 1985)

27. *An Introduction to the New Testament*, D. Carson, D. Moo, L. Morris, (Leicester: Apollos, 1992).

28. *Themes in Old Testament Theology*, William Dyrness, (Leicester; IVP, 1979).

29. *Towards an Old Testament Theology*, Walter Kaiser, (Zondervan, 1991).

30. *New Testament Theology*, Donald Guthrie, (Leicester: IVP, 1981).

31. *A Theology of the New Testament*, G.E. Ladd, (Lutterworth, 1991).

32. *New Testament Theology*, Leon Morris, (Academic Books, 1986).

33. *Systematic Theology*, Wayne Grudem, (Leicester: IVP, 1994).

34. *Systematic Theology*, Louis Berkhof, (Banner of Truth, 1966).

35. *Know the Truth*, Bruce Milne, (Leicester: IVP, 1995).

36. *The Evangelical Faith*, Helmut Thielicke, (Edinburgh: T&T Clarke, 1997).

37. *Christian Theology*, Millard Erickson, (Baker, 1985).

38. *Peoples of the Old Testament World*, A. Hoerth G. Mattingh E. Yamauchi, (Baker, 1994).

39. *Giving Goliath his Due*, Neal Bierling, (Baker, 1992).

40. *Sketches of Jewish Social Life*, Alfred Edersheim, (Eerdmans, 1990).

41. *God's People in God's Land*, Christopher Wright, (Eerdmans 1990).

42. *Christianity in the Hellenistic World*, Roland Nash, (Zondervan, 1984).

43. *Manners & Customs of Bible Times*, Ralph Gower, (Moody, 1987).

44. *The Book of Acts in its First Century Setting*, Ed. Bruce Winter & Andrew Clarke, (Eerdmans, 1993).

45. *Protestant Biblical Interpretation*, Bernard Ramm, (Baker, 1997.

46. *How to Read the Bible as Literature*, Leland Ryken, (Academic Books, 1984).

47. *How to Read the Bible for all its Worth*, Gordon Fee & Douglas Stuart, (Milton Keynes: Scripture Union, 1983).

48. *Introduction to Biblical Interpretation*, W. Klein C.Blomberg R. Hubbard, (Word, 1993)

49. *How to Read the Psalms*, Tremper Longman III, (IVP, 1988).

50. *The Wisdom of Proverbs*, Job & Ecclesiastes, Derek Kidner, (Leicester: IVP, 1985).

51. *Interpreting the Parables*, Craig Blomberg, (Leicester: Apollos, 1990).

52. *Word Biblical Commentaries*, Ed.,   (Word Books,).

53. *Word Biblical Commentary*, (Word Books, 1985).

54. *New International Commentary on the Old Testament* Ed., (Eerdmans).

55. *New International Commentary on the New Testament*, Ed., (Eerdmans).

56. *New international Greek Text Commentary*, Ed., Howard Marshall, (Eerdmans).

57. *The Pillar Commentary*, Ed. Don Carson, (Eerdmans, Apollos).

58. *Tyndale Old/New Testament Commentary*, Ed. D.J. Wiseman & Leon Morris, (Leicester: IVP).
59. *The Bible Speaks Today*, Ed.J.A. Motyer & John Stott, (Leicester: IVP).
60. *Daily Study Bible*, St Andrews Press.

Chapter 9
1. Haddon Robinson, *Expository Preaching*, p.39, (Leicester: IVP, 1999).
2. Romans 5:1,2.

Chapter 12
1. Galatians 1:16 New American Standard Version.

BIBLIOGRAPHY

AZURDIA III, Arturo, *Spirit Empowered Preaching*, (Tain: Mentor, 1998).

ADAM, Peter, *Speaking God's Words*, (Leicester: IVP, 1996).

BAINTON, Roland, *Here I Stand*, (London: Lion, 1988)

BAXTER, Richard, *The Reformed Pastor*, (Edinburgh: Banner of Truth, 1997)

BLACK, James, *The Mystery of Preaching*, (Marshall, Morgan & Scott, 1977).

BLOMBERG, Craig, *Interpreting the Parables*, (Leicester: Apollos, 1990).

CALVIN, John, *Institutes of the Christian Religion*, (Battles trans., Westminster).

CARSON, Don, *Exegetical Fallacies*, (London: Baker, 1989).

DILLARD, R and LONGMAN, T, *An Introduction to the Old Testament*, (Leicester: Apollos, 1995).

EUSEBIUS, *The History of the Church*, (Dorset, 1965).

EZELL, Rick, *Hitting a Moving Target*, (Kregel, 1999).

FACT FILE 2000Carel Press, 2000.

FEE, Gordon, *1&2 Timothy*, (NIBC, Hendrickson, 1990)

FEE, G and STUART, D, *How to Read the Bible for all its Worth*, (Milton Keynes: Scripture Union, 1989).

HILL, Andrew and Walton, John, *A Survey of the Old Testament*, (Zondervan, 1991).

HUGHES, Philip, *The Book of Revelation*, (Leicester: IVP, 1990).

JENKINS, Trica, *Media, Communication and Production*, (Focal Press, 1977).

KIDNER, Derek, *The Wisdom of Proverbs, Job & Ecclesiastes*, (Leicester: IVP, 1985).

KLEIN, W, HUBBARD, R & BLOMBERG, C.
Introduction to Biblical Interpretation, (Word, 1993).

LANE, Denis, *Preach the Word*, (Evangelical Press, 1986).

LARSEN, D, *The Anatomy of Preaching*, (Kregal, 1989).

LINCOLN, Andrew, *Ephesians*, (WBC, Word, 1990).

LONGMAN, T, *How to Read the Psalms*, (Leicester: IVP, 1988).

MARTYR, Justin, *First Apology, The Anti-Nicene Fathers, Vol.1*, (Eerdmans, 1993).

NORRINGTON, D, *To Preach or not to Preach*, (Paternoster Press, 1996).

O'BRIEN, Peter, *Commentary on Philippians*, NIGTC, (Eerdmans, 1991).

OSBORNE, Grant, *The Hermeneutical Spiral*, (Leicester: IVP, 1990).

POLLOCK, John, *George Whitefield*, (Lion 1991).

PACKER, James, *Among God's Giants*, (Kingsway, 1991)

RAMM, Bernard, *Protestant Biblical Interpretation*, (Baker, 1970).

ROBINSON, H, *Expository Preaching*, (Leicester: IVP, 1999).

RYKEN, Leland, *How To Read the Bible as Literature*, (Academic Books, 1984).

SARGENT, Tony, *The Sacred Anointing*, (Hodder & Stoughton, 1994).

SOCIAL TRENDS 28, Office for National Statistics, The Stationary Office, 1998 edition .

STOTT, John, *I Believe in Preaching*, (Hodder, 1982).

VANGEMEREN, W, *Interpreting the Prophetic Word*, (Zondervan, 1990).

VIRKLER, Henry, *Hermeneutics*, (Baker, 1981).

WWW.barb.co.uk/tvfacts/story.cfm

Other books of interest
from Christian Focus

Expository Preaching With Word Pictures
Jack Hughes
With Illustrations from the
Sermons of Thomas Watson

This rich study should be a treasure in every preacher's library. I highly recommend it.'
Dr Richard Mayhue, Sr. Vice President and Dean, The Master's Seminary

In a society dominated by multi-media presentations in full Technicolor Jack Hughes tells that there is no hiding place for the lazy preacher who is contented to preach in monochrome. The days of preaching with all the 'fervour of a weather-forecaster' must surely be behind us!'
David Meredith, Smithton Free Church of Scotland, Inverness

'I have over three hundred volumes on preaching in my library, but only a few of them offer anything so instructive, fresh and interesting. Hughes' book adds significantly to that small number.'
Jay E. Adams, Enoree, South Carolina

'In our image-saturated society, effective preachers who fail to reach the imagination of their listeners will never touch their hearts and move their wills. With the sermons of Thomas Watson as Exhibit A, the author shows you how to use a sanctified imagination to bring meaningful "pictures" out of the text and into your sermons, without sacrificing biblical content or homiletical structure.'
Warren W. Wiersbe, Author and Conference Speaker

Dr. Jack Hughes is pastor-teacher of Calvary Bible Church in Burbank, California. Jack received his Master of Divinity degree from The Master's Seminary, Sun Valley California and his Doctorate of Ministry degree from Westminster Theological Seminary in Escondido, California.

ISBN 1 85792 658 7

The Power of Speaking God's Word
How to preach memorable sermons
Wilbur Ellsworth

Wilbur Ellsworth, after twenty-five years of preaching, started investigating why some sermons had a greater impact than others. Could an over reliance on notes be a factor? Would a lack of notes lead to shallowness, clichés and repetition? Surely doctrinal preaching needed more than his memory could provide?

"Ellsworth's book has been good for my soul and my preaching. It is a pleasure to commend this fine book." **R. Kent Hughes, College Church, Wheaton, Illinois**

"Dr. Ellsworth preaches to large congregations and provides moving testimony to how his preaching changed positively when he weaned himself from an addiction to his manuscript... highly recommended for all students and practitioners of the craft." **Dr. David Larsen, Trinity Evangelical Divinity School**.

"Preaching without notes: I've watched the idea strike terror onto the hearts of fledgling preachers - and not a few veterans - countless times. But now there is help. Wilbur Ellsworth shows not only that this feat can be done, but also, more importantly, how and why it should be done." **Dr. Duane Litfin, President, Wheaton College**

"Most preachers have been taught to produce carefully written material to be given in the pulpit. Changing patterns is hard but Wilbur Ellsworth will show you why you should change and how you can. His thoughts have deeply impacted my own preaching," **Dr. John H. Armstrong, President, Reformation & Revival Ministries**

Dr. Wilbur Ellsworth, a graduate of Ithaca College (New York), Los Angeles Baptist Theological Seminary and Trinity Evangelical Divinity School, has pastored for thirty years in three states and presently lives in Wheaton, Illinois.

ISBN 1 85792 604 8

Power Preaching for Church Growth
The role of preaching in growing churches
David Eby

Filled with much sound wisdom and Biblical insight, it is a gentle wake-up call not only for the Church Growth Movement, but also for my church and for yours.
John MacArthur, President, The Master's Seminary

Dave Eby has put his finger onsomething very crucial, namely the absence of any emphasis on preaching in the Church Growth Movement. This absence is a great concern to me and I believe it is to many who believe that the word of God is the power of God unto salvation. **John Piper, Bethlehem Baptist Church, Minneapolis**

Having been formally trained in the teaching and practice of the Church Growth Movement, I am keenly aware of the good intentions and goals of may who embrace this philosophy for the church. I heavily used Church Growth thinking in my early pastoral labors. When I came to see that the Word of God was authority for both message and method, I was forced to re-evaluate this movement. David Eby's very excellent book would have helped me immeasurably. **John Armstrong, Reformation and Revival**

Dave Eby is not only well-qualified to tackle this subject because of his extensive training, research and pastoral experience; he is also a man with a pastor's heart, deeply commited to feeding Christ's sheep the Word of Life. His passion for God and his truth is matched by his passion for people, so one will not find this book a pedantic critique. His constructive criticism of the Church Growth Movement points us to a better way forward - the approach of the book of Acts. **Michael Horton, Christians United for Reformation**

David Eby is pastor of North City Presbyterian Church in San Diego. He has studied hundreds of volumes of literature of the Church Growth Movement, is commited to the goal of church growth, and leads the lively ministry team of a growing church in California.

ISBN 1 85792 2522

Preaching the Living Word
Addresses from the Evangelical Ministry Assembly
Edited by David Jackman

**Dick Lucas, Alec Motyer, J.I. Packer,
Bruce Milne, Peter Jensen,
David Jackman, Mark Ashton**

*'These superb addresses are the pick of the crop.
They are absolute gold dust. I recommend this
book enthusiastically and with joy.'*
Wallace Benn, Bishop of Lewes

'
*This compilation of carefully edited addresses is an excellent
sampler of the Assembly itself. More than that it provides the kind of
instructive teaching and preaching which will serve to strengthen the
ministry of the Word of God everywhere.'*
**Dr. Sinclair B. Ferguson,
St George's Tron Parish Church, Glasgow**

*'This excellent book is a joy to read... it wonderfully captures the feel
of the assembly'*
Dr. Paul Gardner, Rural Dean, Hartford, Cheshire

In this book you will discover:-
- How to make preaching more effective
- How to restore it's centrality to worship in the Church
- How to structure Bible exposition
- How to preach from different parts of Scripture
- How to preach doctrine

This is not a book about style, but how to extract the best from
the Word of God when delivering a message.

ISBN 1 85792 312X